SIMPLE

Christians

SIMPLY
Christians

NEW TESTAMENT
CHRISTIANITY
IN THE
21ST CENTURY

SAM E. STONE

COLLEGE PRESS PUBLISHING COMPANY · JOPLIN, MISSOURI

Cover design by Mark Cole

Library of Congress Cataloging-in-Publication Data

Stone, Sam E.
   Simply Christians: New Testament Christianity in the 21st century / by Sam
E. Stone.
       p.   cm.
   Includes bibliographical references.
   ISBN 0-89900-489-X (pbk.)
   1. Churches of Christ—Doctrines.   2. Restoration movement (Christianity).
I. Title.
   BX7077.S76 2004
   286.6—dc22

                                                                    2004013362

A C K N O W L E D G M E N T S

Every author is a debtor. Many people contribute to the writing of most books. This one is no exception.

I am grateful to the team at College Press—and especially to Mark Moore who first challenged me to address the topic, and to Dru Ashwell who shepherded me through the months of writing and rewriting.

Knowledgeable friends like Victor Knowles, Chris DeWelt, Jim North, Walter Birney, Lyndsay Jacobs and Doug Priest all provided valuable insights. Woody Wilkinson offered his assistance and introduced me to one of his students at Ozark Christian College, Mark Wall, who helped in the early research. Ronnie Cordrey and Chris Travis provided helpful illustrations. Don Waddell made available valuable research on the current status of megachurches.

My former colleagues at Standard Publishing went beyond the call of duty in sharing resources from past issues of *Christian Standard*. Editor and Publisher Mark Taylor graciously granted permission for us to reprint several important pieces in their entirety. Ruth Davis and Jim Nieman were extremely helpful, as was Margaret Williams, my computer guru. David Faust encouraged me in the use of the title "Simply Christians," one that he had chosen for a special edition of *The Lookout* some years ago.

Both of my sons provided wise counsel, steadfast prayer, and much-needed encouragement, as did my most faithful supporter, my wife Gwen. Her brother, Lynn Gardner, helped me to focus on the theme, and gave practical help with the organization, the approach, and the writing of the book.

DEDICATION

I have always found Lynn Gardner's counsel invaluable. He has given me wise advice in every job I have had since college days. I value what he says, and I appreciate the thoughtful way in which he says it. His unassuming manner, his plain speaking, and his ability to clarify issues—these are treasures. To me, he is more than my brother-in-law; he is as close as any brother could be. With appreciation and affection, this book is dedicated to him.

TABLE OF CONTENTS

INTRODUCTION

They must be doing something right! That's how one Christian leader put it when he observed the remarkable growth and vitality among Christian Churches and Churches of Christ. This book suggests some possible reasons why this may be happening.

WHO SHOULD USE THE BOOK?

This book will be helpful to at least three groups of people:

1. Those who have never heard of the "Restoration Movement." This fast-growing, 19th-century effort sought to unite believers and evangelize the world by teaching and practicing the Christianity of the New Testament. The book introduces readers to Christian Churches and Churches of Christ which continue to share this vision.
2. Those who know a *little* about this fellowship of churches, but want to learn *more*. Resources for further study are suggested in the Bibliography and the Appendix.
3. Those who want an up-to-date look at the latest available facts and figures, along with a review of the basic principles of the Restoration Movement.

WHO ARE WE TALKING ABOUT?

In today's church landscape, three identifiable church groups share a common heritage in the Restoration Movement.[1]

Christian Churches and *Churches of Christ.* (They use the two names interchangeably.) The focus of this book is on this fellowship of congregations. They are congregational in government and conservative in theology. The *Directory of the Ministry* publishes an annual listing of them (see Bibliography).

Churches of Christ. These congregations prefer the term "Church of Christ" to describe themselves. In addition, they normally use only a cappella music, without instrumental accompaniment. These churches are also congregational in government and conservative in theology. While most of them share common beliefs with the congregations described in this book, they are listed separately in the U.S. Census and elsewhere. Although we have much in common with these churches, we will not attempt to include a full report of their current activities and accomplishments in this book.

Disciples of Christ. Another group of congregations with historic ties to the Restoration Movement are the Christian Churches identified as Disciples of Christ. These churches are structured as a denomination with a centralized headquarters. The theological position of the Disciples of Christ is generally more liberal than the churches described in this book, but they nevertheless trace their roots to the same heritage.

WHAT WILL YOU FIND?

Few people have convenient access to accurate, up-to-date information about the Christian Churches and Churches of Christ, nor all of the varied projects and organizations they sponsor. One of the goals for this book is to bring together as much current data as possible in order to facilitate research and cooperative efforts. Chapter Two focuses especially on current statistics.

These churches are not structured under a central denominational headquarters, but rather function as self-governing local congregations. Because of this, no one is compelled to fill out surveys, send in reports, or respond to queries for information about a church or other organization. All of the information in this book is as current and as accurate as we could make it.

Members of these churches may appreciate a summary of the heritage and convictions that mark these congregations. The second section of the book is intended to provide such an overview.

ENDNOTES

1. The World Convention of Churches of Christ is an umbrella organization that provides a place of contact and fellowship for folk from all three groups, as well as with nationals from scores of countries around the world who share a common faith and heritage. The Bibliography lists their Web site for those who want more information.

PART *One*

WHO ARE
THESE PEOPLE?

1

UNDERSTANDING THE GOAL

*T*he *New York Times* for September 18, 2002 reported on the growth rate of religious groups with one million or more adherents. Many were surprised to learn that the second fastest-growing religious group in America over the past 10 years was the fellowship of Christian Churches and Churches of Christ. Between 1990 and 2000, these churches increased by 18.6 percent. That fact should not have been surprising. The primary goal of these churches resonates with many people.

In today's religious world, people are tired of fighting over inconsequential details. They are impatient with partisan bickering and constant complaining. They want to see an inclusive fellowship, reaching out to all. They are ready to see lives that match liturgy, people who practice what they preach. It is "back to basics" time.

The church of the Lord Jesus Christ is just what people want and need.

Not some "official" church.

Not a powerful, political church.

But just *the church*. Christ's church. The church we read about in Scripture.

In the New Testament church, people loved each other. They taught truth, not what is politically correct. Kindness and respect characterized their evangelistic efforts. They insisted only on obedience to the plain commands of Jesus.

On the surface, this might seem easy, even simplistic. In many cases, Church has gotten complicated over the last 2000 years. People think that a "real church" requires a denominational hierarchy and headquarters from which big-name speakers are promoted, policies are dictated, dues and other funds are collected, polling statistics are tabulated, issues are debated, resolutions are documented and beliefs are legislated.

A BETTER WAY

For at least 200 years, some believers have said, "There has to be a better way." And they have demonstrated that there is. Christians don't have to perpetuate a divided denominational church. We don't have to separate into warring sects, each clustered around a person or a position, a creed or a confession. The only affirmation of faith in the days of the early church was, "I believe that Jesus is the Christ, the Son of the living God." If that statement was good enough in Bible days, it is good enough now.

These believers insist on no more than Scripture requires: a person is free to accept God's grace by obedient faith in Christ; encouraged to turn from sin in repentance; helped to demonstrate and mark his or her choice to identify with Christ through baptism; supported in the daily process of learning to live for Jesus. This perspective reflects the primary goal of the Christian Churches—trusting God and His Word as the perfect guide for every aspect of faith and faithful living (2 Peter 1:3).

Believers assemble with others in local congregations. Servant leaders help the body to evangelize the community and disciple followers. Elders oversee and shepherd the flock. Evangelists, pastors, and teachers—all gifted by God—minister in various ways. Some may be more prominent and visible, but there is no clergy/laity distinction. No organizational ties exist beyond the local church. No hierarchy. No denominational headquarters. Broad cooperation in benevolent, evangelistic, and educational outreach certainly occurs, however.

These folks want to work together with all who accept the lordship of Jesus and the authority of His Word. People don't have to see eye-to-eye on every detail, or agree on the interpretation of every Bible verse to cooperate in worthwhile projects. In the essentials of the faith, they insist on unity; in matters of opinion, they allow liberty; and in all things they seek to show love.

Many of those who are trying to live out this conviction also join together to worship in Christian Churches and Churches of Christ.[1] These congregations are part of what has been called a "Restoration Movement." This is because they seek to *restore* the kind of Christianity practiced in the New Testament. This book is intended to introduce you to those of us who are a part of this movement.

Thousands of earnest believers have identified with this approach over the years. They have decided to be known simply as *Christians,* without any extra descriptive label. They follow only Scripture as their source of authority. They work together in voluntary, free associations, but without any denominational structure or man-made rules. This approach has proved workable, and God has blessed it! In the 21st century, millions of Christ's followers around the globe echo a key Restoration Movement slogan, "We are not the only Christians, but we *are* Christians only."

We don't want to set ourselves apart from any other believers. We don't feel we are better, or smarter, or holier than any other believer. We want to learn how to be more like Christ wants us to be. We want to share the biblical truths that we've learned with everyone we can. Moreover, we want to learn along with others all that our Lord expects of us.

Since Jesus is the only hope of salvation, and since the biggest part of the world doesn't know Him yet, we realize our work is cut out for us. Missions is not just a part of our work—it is the *heart* of it. A lost world needs Jesus!

In brief, that's the goal being pursued by thousands of Christian Churches and Churches of Christ today.

Why am I a member of the Church of Christ? Because I believe independent Churches of Christ and Christian Churches— "Restoration" churches—get to the point.

A VALID APPROACH

Ralph Kinney Bennett has served for years as an elder in one of these congregations. A longtime senior editor of *Reader's Digest*, Bennett explained why he is a part of this movement in a widely-circulated article that first appeared in *Christian Standard*.[2]

He writes:

"What church are you with?"
"Christian."
"No, I mean what denomination?"
"Christian. We just call ourselves Christians."
"Oh."
I could not begin to count how many times I have engaged in such an exchange. . . . By insisting that Christians should call themselves just that, Alexander Campbell[3] clearly signaled a return to fundamentals and equipped us with a marvelous intellectual "foot in the door."
Once we begin to explain why we call ourselves "Christians only," once we introduce the biblical foundation, the logic, the simplicity of it,

we have opened the way to the very roots and heart of what the church was and is still supposed to be. It is the body of Christ on earth and it is supposed to be—*despite* all the well-intentioned additions and accretions we humans have put upon it—nothing more or less than spiritually reborn people worshiping God and living—simply—by His Word.

If I had to describe in one phrase the whole body of what the Campbells sought, it would be "get to the point." When Paul preached in Athens, he got to the point. When Stephen spoke before the Sanhedrin, he got to the point. When Jesus conversed with the woman at the well, He got to the point.

They strive to remove all the man-made clutter which threatens to get between me and my own personal experience of relationship with and worship of the Lord. In that, they cleave to the New Testament ideal. That ideal is characterized by simplicity.

Not surprisingly a lot of people see the validity of this approach. They too want to get back to basics. They are tired of "playing church." They are turned off by powerful religious institutions which seem to have forgotten that the church was intended to be focused on Christ's own priority, to seek and save the lost.

Many are weary of debating minuscule points of doctrine, while neglecting care, compassion, and comfort for hurting humanity. They find it refreshing to find people who sincerely attempt to reproduce the kind of Christianity first seen after Jesus established His church on the Day of Pentecost (Acts 2).[4]

They are delighted to find genuine Christians trying to live out their faith in a fallen world. All of us need help as we try to do that. Some say, "It takes a village to raise a child." For sure it takes a church to raise a Christian! There is no "Lone Ranger mentality" in the church pictured in the New Testament.

Instead, God's people are compared to parts of the human body— closely connected to each other and to the head, Christ. When life falls apart, we quickly realize that we must depend upon the Lord and His people. That is where Christ's church comes in. Each congregation seeks to live up to the family ideal described in Scripture.

In saying this, we don't mean that those of us who try to do this are perfect. Far from it. We know many of our shortcomings and imperfections all too well. We have not "arrived," but we are confident that this approach is the right way to recapture and reproduce Christianity in its original form in today's world. If this makes sense to you, keep reading!

ENDNOTES

1. These two names can be used interchangeably.
2. Ralph Kinney Bennett, "Why I Am a Member of the Church of Christ." This article first appeared in *Christian Standard*, November 14, 1993. It is now available in a special reprint, *What Kind of Church Is This?* That reprint and other helpful resources for those wanting an introduction to Restoration Movement churches are listed in the Appendix.
3. Alexander Campbell (1788–1866) was one of the most prominent leaders as the Restoration Movement began. With his father Thomas, he encouraged churches to reform themselves in the light of Scripture.
4. Two summaries of basic convictions of those in this fellowship are also included in the Appendix. The first was written by former President James A. Garfield, a leader in these churches in the 1800s. The second is by a contemporary leader, Dr. Lynn Gardner, longtime dean of Ozark Christian College. Both are simple and direct, answering questions often asked about the churches.

2

CONSIDERING

THE EVIDENCE

The validity of any movement must first be tested by its conformity to truth. Are the things taught in harmony with God's Word? In the six chapters of Part Two ("What Do They Believe?"), we attempt to demonstrate that they are. The core values of the Christian Churches and Churches of Christ are outlined in that section.

But it is also appropriate to see how God has blessed the efforts of those committed to restoring New Testament Christianity today. To get to know these people who seek to be "simply Christians," it may be helpful to look at what those *outside* of the movement say about them.

If these churches are following biblical principles—and we believe they are—it should come as no surprise that they are enjoying both numerical and spiritual growth. Consider five examples of this.

> **When people speak the truth in love and seek to practice basic Christianity, God blesses with vibrant growth.**

1. THE GLENMARY STUDY

The *New York Times* article cited in chapter 1 provides an unbiased, objective view of this fellowship.[1] In a copyrighted article (September 18, 2002), "Conservative Churches Grew Fastest in 1990's, Report Says," Laurie Goodstein wrote,

Socially conservative churches that demand high commitment from their members grew faster than other religious denominations in the last decade, according to a study released yesterday by statisticians who count American religious affiliations every 10 years.

The study, *Religious Congregations and Membership 2000*, found that the fastest-growing religious denomination in the last 10 years was the Church of Jesus Christ of Latter-day Saints, which enlists thousands of young Mormon missionaries to recruit door to door and boosted its membership in the United States by 19.3 percent to a total of 4.2 million since the last survey in 1990.

The denominations that recorded the next highest growth were the conservative Christian Churches and Churches of Christ, with 18.6 percent; the Assemblies of God, a major Pentecostal denomination with 18.5 percent; and the Roman Catholic Church, with 16.2 percent.

The author went on to note the significance of this study. "Because the Census Bureau does not ask about religion, some scholars regard this study, first done in 1971, as the most comprehensive assessment available of the changes in American religious affiliation."

The Glenmary Institute Study confirmed and highlighted the growth enjoyed by the Restoration Movement in recent years.

Some may suggest that the figures in the Glenmary study are not totally accurate because the researchers include children who attend, but are not yet baptized members in the churches. While it is true that the researchers included a reasonable estimate of younger children in finalizing their head count, this was only done so that interested observers could compare "apples to apples."[2]

In the Roman Catholic church, for example, infants are counted as members. In Christian Churches they are not. But every week multiplied thousands of infants and young children are in attendance in those same Christian Churches. While the little children are not yet members, they *are* a part of the constituency of these congregations. Therefore, when the Glenmary Institute chose to compare the total number of people attending Roman Catholic churches with the total number attending Christian Churches, this basis seems reasonable. The same formula was followed with all other religious groups, including the a cappella Churches of Christ.[3]

The Glenmary Institute study reports a total of 5,471 congregations for the Christian Churches and Churches of Christ, with 1,156,699 "full members" and an estimated 1,439,253 "adherents."[4] These churches increased in membership by 226,065 between 1990 and 2000, according to the report. During the same time, the total number of Christian Church congregations increased by 233.

In the *New York Times* article announcing results of the study, the director of Glenmary Research Center observed, "I was astounded to see that by and large the growing churches are those that we ordinarily call conservative." Ken Sanchagrin added, "And when I looked at those that were declining, most were moderate or liberal churches. And the more liberal the denomination, by most people's definition, the more they were losing."[5]

The *Directory of the Ministry* provides the most complete listing of congregations and personnel for this fellowship. The latest edition reports a total of 5,480 churches with a membership of 1,199,048 people (2003 edition).[6]

By whatever measure one uses to estimate the size of this group of churches attempting to restore New Testament Christianity today, they are obviously growing steadily. Some of the other reasons for this increase may become evident as we continue.

2. FOREIGN MISSIONARIES

Next it is appropriate to consider some of the facts and figures that mark specific areas of growth in the Christian Churches and Churches of Christ. Take foreign missions, for example.

The health and vitality of any group of churches may be understood better by observing their efforts in world evangelism. In this area as in others, it is difficult to get a precise, accurate head count of all the missionaries sent out from Christian Churches and Churches of Christ. There is no one central agency to which all must report, since this nondenominational fellowship has no hierarchy.

One of the most respected resources for information in the field of missions, however, is the *Mission Handbook*. It is published by Evangelism and Missions Information Service at the Billy Graham Center of Wheaton College. According to their most recent edition, the Christian Churches and Churches of Christ have 1154 missionaries sent out from the U.S., making them the third largest sending group among all Protestants.[7]

The *Mission Handbook* indicates the Southern Baptists have the largest group with 4562 workers, the Assemblies of God are next with 1543, followed by the Christian Churches with 1154. The a cappella Churches of Christ are fourth in size, with 1014 missionaries.

The major gathering that focuses on world evangelism among Christian Churches and Churches of Christ is the National Missionary Convention. It meets annually in various cities across the U.S. The longtime executive director, Walter Birney, estimates that there are well over 1,000 missionaries overseas sponsored by these churches, with at least that many more doing some kind of mission work here in the United States.

The following statistics from some of the larger sending organizations of the Christian Churches confirm this as a reasonable estimate. For example, the Christian Missionary Fellowship presently has 195 missionaries involved in overseas work; Team Expansion presently has 240; Pioneer Bible Translators has another 135.[8] Hundreds more are supported directly by churches.

These figures do *not* include the hundreds of American Christians who annually take short-term mission trips to various fields. Many others work with "home missions" (within the United States) including various evangelizing fellowships, benevolent, and special outreach efforts (such as to youth, people with disabilities, various ethnic groups, and others).

In addition, some are doing mission work in restricted countries, and do not publicize their activity for fear this might jeopardize the work and their own safety. In still other areas where U.S.-sent missionaries would not be welcome, nationals from other countries are sending out their own workers to preach and teach in these restricted lands.

3. CHRISTIAN HIGHER EDUCATION

From the earliest days of the Restoration Movement, Christian higher education has been a paramount emphasis. Alexander Campbell founded Bethany College (Bethany, West Virginia) in 1840. In the ensuing years, many other schools sprang up to train Christian leaders.

Over the past century, Bible colleges have been especially strong. These institutions are dedicated to providing a rounded undergraduate education, with special emphasis on both biblical content and practical ministries. The national accrediting association for these schools is the Accrediting Association of Bible Colleges.[9] In that organization, schools sponsored by the Christian Churches and Churches of Christ play an important role.

In 2000, for example, a total of 87 Bible colleges were accredited by the AABC. Of this figure, the largest number of schools from any religious group were the 16 from the Christian Churches. By way of comparison, 17 schools were affiliated with *all* of the various Baptist denominations (7 were Independent Baptists, the rest from other Baptist groups), 5 were Wesleyan, and 4 Assembly of God.

The annual College Issue of *Christian Standard* profiled 36 schools in the March 21, 2004, edition. This report includes liberal arts colleges and seminaries as well as Bible colleges.[10]

4. New Church Plants

Another factor in the dramatic growth of the Restoration Movement in the past decade has been new church planting. A grassroots effort known as "Double Vision" began back in the 1980s to encourage the establishment of new congregations around the country. Peter Wagner, a well-known and respected church growth expert, has observed that the most effective way to grow the kingdom is to start a new church. Statistics confirm that this is one of the best ways to reach new people with the gospel. Many more unchurched folks will visit a *new* congregation rather than an existing one.

Across America, new church planting has blossomed in the Restoration Movement. While we have been unable to compile an all-inclusive total of the number of new churches begun, we learned of several exemplary efforts. Here are some examples from various parts of the country over the years 1993–2003:

Northern California Evangelistic Association
    53 new churches started; average weekly attendance now—15,500
Go Ye Chapel Mission (now Orchard Group), New York City
    9 new churches started; average weekly attendance now—3,085
Chicago District Evangelizing Association
    10 new churches started; average weekly attendance now—2400
Christian Evangelizing Fellowship (Cincinnati, Ohio)
    12 new churches started; average weekly attendance now—2500
Christian Evangelistic Association (The Northwest)
    6 new churches started; average weekly attendance now—600

5. Megachurches

Each year *Christian Standard* publishes the average attendance, number of baptisms and transfers of membership from all of the known megachurches (congregations that average 1,000 or more attending weekend services). For the year 2003, a total of 97 churches were reported.[11] After the report was published (March 7, 2004), 5 more congregations were reported! This makes a total of 102 confirmed megachurches. These larger congregations provide significant leadership in the wider world of Christianity as well as within this fellowship of churches. Some believe that more megachurches exist among the Christian Churches and Churches of Christ than any other group of churches today.

The dramatic growth of these megachurches, combined with the other factors cited, give evidence of the attractiveness of simple nondenominational Christianity. When people speak the truth in love and seek to practice basic Christianity, God blesses with vibrant growth.

Bob Russell ministers with Southeast Christian Church, Louisville, Kentucky—the largest church in this fellowship and one of the ten largest churches in the United States of *any* group.[12] He wrote, "God is using our simple, nondenominational plea to reach people. What Alexander Campbell, Thomas Campbell, Barton W. Stone and others dreamed of, we are experiencing right now! . . . An official from the Navigators asked me what was going on in our movement. He said, 'All over America, I am seeing more vibrancy in the Christian Church than any other movement.' It is not just large churches; great things are happening in smaller churches, with new-church plants, in parachurch organizations, Bible colleges, and missions work."[13]

Victor Knowles, editor of *One Body*, analyzed the growth of Christian Churches and Churches of Christ in a lecture at Pepperdine University, April 30, 2003.[14] He concluded, "If we will pursue the leading of the Spirit, the coming decades have the potential to be the best in our fellowship in a century and a half. May His church grow!"

ENDNOTES

1. *The New York Times*, September 18, 2002, A-22.

2. *Religious Congregations and Membership in the United States, 2000*, xv. This report is copyrighted by the Association of Statisticians of American Religious Bodies (2002) and is published by Glenmary Research Center, 1212 Fifth Avenue North, Nashville, TN 37208. Researchers who analyzed results for the Glenmary study explain, "In an effort to achieve comparability of date, major categories were established:
   1. Members, 2. Total Adherents. The staff estimated total adherents for the 67 groups that reported members only, following a formula they devised. They felt "this would be as nearly equitable and accurate as possible."

3. Ibid., 2. The most recent available figures for the a cappella Churches of Christ is 13,027 congregations with 1,264,808 members. Other data on these churches is available in Mac Lynn's *Churches of Christ in the U. S. (2000 edition)* (Nashville: 21st Century Christian, 2000), 31.

4. Ibid., p. 1

5. *The New York Times*, op. cit.

6. *Directory of the Ministry (2003 edition)*, ed. by Judy Noll, (Springfield, Ill., Specialized Christian Services, 2003) 46.

7. *Mission Handbook*, 2001–2003 edition, ed. by John A. Siewert and Dotsey Welliver (Wheaton, Ill.: Evangelism and Missions Information Service, 2003) 51, 52.

8. Each group has its own way of listing workers. Christian Missionary Fellowship reports 124 missionaries on the field; 45 recruits raising funds to go; and about 25 people on staff in Indianapolis. Team Expansion has 240 full-timers, including husbands and wives; this includes 27 in the International Office, many of whom are focused on fields. Pioneer Bible Translators has 101 adult missionaries with 34 in active training who have full recruit status; in addition, there are 95 children.

9. The Accrediting Association of Bible Colleges changed its name on June 1, 2004, to Commission on Accreditation of the Association for Biblical Higher Education.

10. The copyrighted Christian College Issue chart from the March 21, 2004, issue of *Christian Standard* is reprinted in the Appendix by permission of Standard Publishing.

11. The complete consolidated megachurch list from *Christian Standard* is also available in the Appendix. The reports from both the March 7, 2004, and April 25, 2004, issues are included in this one single list.

12. The ranking of Southeast Christian Church among the top ten can be verified from two independent sources:

    1. The Hartford Institute.
        Web site: **http://hirr.hartsem.edu/org/faith_megachurches_database.html**
    2. Forbes magazine.
        Web site: **http://www.forbes.com/2003/09/17/cz_lk_0917megachurch.html**

13. Bob Russell, "Six Reasons Why We Need the NACC!" *Christian Standard*, April 27, 2003.

14. Victor Knowles, "Analyze This—Why Conservative Christian Churches/Churches of Christ Were the Second Fastest Growing Church in America From 1990–2000," 60th Annual Pepperdine University Bible Lectures, April 30, 2003. This material is available on the Web and may be viewed at this site: **www.poeministries.org**.

3

THE
ACCEPTING
CHALLENGE

Those seeking to reproduce New Testament Christianity today have a worthy goal. As we have shown in the previous chapter, their efforts are being blessed by God. While these signs of growth are encouraging, they are not an occasion to brag, nor to rest on past accomplishments.

While the Christian Churches and Churches of Christ have had significant growth, we must remember that a cult—the Latter Day Saints (Mormons)—grew even faster. The Muslims, too, continue their rapid growth. This is not a time for complacency and self-congratulation.

When the Glenmary Study was first reported, we commented on it in an editorial for *Christian Standard:*

This significant study confirms what many observers had long felt: Christian Churches and Churches of Christ are enjoying strong growth. At the same time, the study serves to underline the challenge before us. As we move into the 21st century, the Great Commission must remain our central concern. The familiar words, "Go ye into all the world," are still the "marching orders" for all who would follow Jesus."[1]

What if we could recapture New Testament Christianity both in what we teach and in how we live? Then people could see that the church now has become what it was then. And what a church it was!

"FOR SUCH A TIME AS THIS"

The plea for New Testament Christianity seems especially appropriate for this generation. Paul Williams, President of Orchard Group and Editor-at-large for *Christian Standard*, declared, "I believe we are the perfect church for the Postmodern age."[2] He went on to explain why:

> The Postmodern age is a time of 500 existing channels, each vying for the right to reality. It is a time of no loyalty to existing structures, a time focused on relationships, and a perfect time for the Restoration Movement. In fact, I believe as people "channel surf" across the various religious channels, they are likely to find us pretty appealing.
>
> First of all, in an age not interested in a thousand different rules and regulations, we know what the core is—the death, burial, and resurrection of Jesus Christ, and the symbols thereof. Our practice of the Lord's Supper and adult baptism are both understood in a Postmodern age, where symbol is highly valued. Our focus on holistic reconciliation of the creation to the Creator also is greatly appreciated in a world that has lost its interest in an understanding of the Christian faith that is too often defined in individualistic terms.
>
> Our understanding of the core of faith is just the beginning. In Margaret Wheatley's *Leadership and the New Science*, she says the "Quantum Age" organization will live within its own boundaries but often leave those boundaries to work synergistically with others. The airlines call it "code sharing." They keep their own identities, but enter into a code-sharing agreement with another airline to work together for the benefit of both. The Restoration Movement's local church independence within a broader body of voluntary cooperation is similar. Each church makes its own decisions, but joins with others when it is in everyone's best interest.

Dick Alexander, president of the 2004 North American Christian Convention, explained the role of the NACC to the congregation where he ministers like this:

> We are part of a nondenominational fellowship of churches numbering about 11,000 congregations worldwide. There's much that's satisfying and productive about being connected to this loose-knit network of churches.
>
> In a free association of churches, there is support and encouragement without bureaucracy. No time and money are wasted oiling denominational machinery. But the synergy of being part of a broader fellowship makes every church stronger.

It's no surprise that this fellowship of churches was the fastest growing in North America during the past decade. Holding core values of adherence to Scripture and commitment to evangelism, the freedom to innovate has produced many exemplary churches and ministries. When we say "loosely" connected, that's accurate. All associations within the fellowship (as well as with groups from other fellowships) are voluntary.

One of the main connecting places for our brotherhood is the North American Christian Convention. It is an annual gathering that provides ideas, inspiration, and identity for the churches, ministries, and their leaders.[3]

RECAPTURING ORIGINAL CHRISTIANITY

The challenge for these churches is to keep before them the New Testament ideal for the church. When the church began back in the first century, the family of God was easy to spot. Christians were recognizable by what they did, as well as by what they said. They walked and worked during the week in ways which were consistent with how they worshiped on Sunday.

The Message, Eugene Peterson's fresh translation of Scripture, describes what took place: "All the believers lived in a wonderful harmony . . . they followed a daily discipline of worship in the Temple followed by meals at home, every meal a celebration, exuberant and joyful, as they praised God. People in general liked what they saw. Every day their number grew as God added those who were saved" (Acts 2:44-47).

Our challenge is to be like the church at its best, as described in the New Testament. In those days unbelievers formed their opinion of the church by watching how Christians lived. "People in general liked what they saw!" People will do the same today! When we show kindness to a neighbor, take time to help a stranger, and offer love to the "unlovely," we demonstrate the reality of our faith. A skeptical world is watching closely.

What if we could recapture New Testament Christianity both in what we teach and in how we live? Then people could see that the church *now* has become what it was *then*. And what a church it was!

The whole congregation of believers was united as one—one heart, one mind. . . . The apostles gave powerful witness to the resurrection of the Master Jesus, and grace was on all of them (Acts 4:32,33, *The Message*).

All over the country—Judea, Samaria, Galilee—the church grew. They were permeated with a deep sense of reverence for God. The Holy Spirit was with them, strengthening them. They prospered wonderfully (Acts 9:31, *The Message*).

What a challenge for us to walk and work and worship our Lord with the same simple, consistent, faithful commitment and integrity!

The future will largely depend on how well those of us committed to the restoration of New Testament Christianity are able to communicate and demonstrate our faith in Jesus. In the second section of this book, six of the most important emphases will be suggested. Years ago Marshall Leggett, former president of Milligan College, offered wise counsel:

> Never has the future looked brighter for the Restoration Movement. Many contemporary believers have experienced disillusionment in the attempt to effect church union by compromise. This has not worked, and, in some instances, has decimated every resemblance to a biblical faith. These same people . . . want to unite with other Christians in a faith centered in Christ and rooted in the Word of God. . . . The Restoration Movement can lead these people to that which they seek.
>
> Attitude on the part of those who comprise the movement will determine much of how effectively Christ will be able to use it. A condemnatory view of others has often manifested itself among those who want to restore the New Testament church. . . . This attitude is both unwarranted and counterproductive, and it contradicts the biblical principle of "speaking the truth in love." One does not have to condemn others in order to be faithful to the restoration ideal. A positive, warm presentation of it will accomplish much more.
>
> An isolationist, exclusionist attitude will likewise be unproductive. The early leaders of the movement never considered themselves as the *only* Christians. That position would necessitate an unwarranted judgmental decision on the part of those who seek to be Christians only. Stone, the Campbells, and Scott looked upon themselves as part of a movement within the church, calling all believers back to the church as it was given to the apostles. . . . The Restoration Movement . . . can respect the integrity of others and rejoice at their good works, as it calls them to unite on a biblical basis.[4]

Dr. Jim North gave a similar appraisal. He spoke of the need to hold both to biblical authority and Christian unity. "How can we do both without jeopardizing or abandoning one or the other?" he asked. Then he answered, "We must avoid being too narrow in the area of biblical authority, while at the same time we avoid being too broad in the area of Christian unity. Perhaps we can say that the more a group reflects proper biblical teaching, the more we can be united with them in Christian activity."[5]

As we do this, we will be upholding the original principles of the Restoration Movement, as outlined by Thomas Campbell in *The Declaration* and *Address.*[6] Of special significance is his statement in the First Proposition, "The church of Christ upon earth is essentially, intentionally, and constitutionally one." If this is true, then we are responsible to do our part to reproduce the church of Scripture as we seek Christian unity in today's world. This is the place to take a stand. By God's grace, we can stand together, meeting the challenge of the gospel in our days, as simply faithful Christians.

RESOLUTIONS

It is time to accept the challenge. Let us make these resolutions:

1. We will try to hold up New Testament Christianity as the ideal. We will urge a return to the scriptural picture of what the church should be, trying to keep the unity of the Spirit in the bond of peace, as we work to win a lost world to Jesus.

2. We will try to keep open the lines of communication with those who disagree with us. We will try to cross lines if that can help achieve these purposes. We will not sit in judgment on sisters or brothers who differ.

3. At the same time, we will not be held prisoner by either the radical right or the liberal left. We will not sell out the principles for applause, will not compromise the goals because of intimidation, and will not forsake the standard of Scripture for some human interpretation of the Scripture.

4. As those who are free in Christ, we want to share as widely as possible the vision that our Restoration forefathers saw. We want to practice the plea. We want to obey the scriptural mandate to speak the truth in love. We may not *always* succeed, but that is what we intend to do. And, what's more, we encourage you to do it, too.

ENDNOTES

1. Sam Stone, "Our Churches Are Growing," *Christian Standard,* November 3, 2002, 3.
2. Paul Williams, "If The Restoration Movement Didn't Exist, We'd Have to Invent It," *Christian Standard,* January 26, 2003.
3. Dick Alexander, "Connecting," *The Connection,* May 13, 2003, Clovernook Christian Church, Cincinnati, 4
4. Marshall Leggett, *Introduction to the Restoration Ideal* (Cincinnati: Standard Publishing, 1986) 218, 219.
5. James B. North, *Union in Truth* (Cincinnati: Standard Publishing, 1994) 366.
6. Thomas Campbell, *The Declaration and Address,* originally printed in 1809 (Birmingham, England: Berean Press, n.d., reprint ed.). All thirteen propositions affirmed by Campbell in this document are reprinted in the Appendix.

PART
Two

WHAT DO
THEY BELIEVE?

4

FOLLOWING JESUS

Lordship of Christ.

J esus is the heart of Christianity. He is our source, our authority, our strength, and our hope. He is Lord. Once Jesus asked His disciples if they also would turn away from Him. Peter responded for them all. "To whom shall we go? You have the words of eternal life. We believe and know that you are the Holy One of God" (John 6:68).

In a world tired of denominational division and debate, it is refreshing to find Christians who simply seek to follow Jesus.

Today in some circles it is considered inappropriate to speak of His exclusive, absolute power. Franklin Graham found this out. At President Bush's inauguration, he mentioned the name of Jesus. Critics quickly said he was intolerant. Franklin Graham explained,

> The Name of Jesus Christ is a lightning rod because Jesus Christ represents the division of life between good and evil, God and Satan, light and darkness, righteousness and sin, heaven and hell. The Name of Jesus shouts out a choice: "Who will you serve, give your life to, depend upon?" Rebellious, self-willed people, sinful people want to retain the right to decide for themselves which way they will take. Jesus denies this option. Speaking on His behalf, the Apostle Peter said, "For there is no other name under heaven given among men by which we must be saved."[1]

The church today must follow Jesus.

The church is built on Jesus Christ. If the church is to be true to Scripture, it must be built on Jesus Christ alone. That's not easy. Even a cursory look at the New Testament reveals that Jesus gave some very specific commands. We dare not ignore them. He deserves our full allegiance. He demands our unconditional surrender.

When the church began, the Christian religion was simple, clear, and basic. Those earliest believers confessed their faith in Christ, putting complete trust in Him. They willingly obeyed His every command. They were loyal, even to the point of death. No wonder that first-century church grew so rapidly!

Now I don't know how you folks feel, but as for me, I'll take what Jesus said! −Brother Don

---

If only we could recapture such commitment today!

The good news is, we can!

Christ is still in the business of transforming lives. Take Troy Newman, a 30-something police officer who lives near Joplin, Missouri. On Easter Sunday, 2002, he told the people at College Heights Christian Church there what had happened in his life:

> I came from a really poor background. I never had anybody really take the time to explain Jesus to me. It kind of made me scared to even want to go to church. Nobody wants to say, "Hey, I'm stupid. Can you help me out?" That's true regardless of what the subject is—but especially when it comes to the Lord. People like me want to think they know enough. They think, "As long as I know *about* Him, then I'm fine," but they're not.
>
> Finally I had someone come into my life who took the time to keep talking to me about Jesus. I had questions I wanted to ask. It was an absolutely amazing feeling. I learned that the Lord is there, that He wants me and needs me. I decided that if there is someone who cares that much about me, He's the one I want to give my life to. I know that I still have a lot of changing to do, but Jesus is everything to me.

Who knows how many more people would come to faith in Christ, if Christians would just talk to them more about Jesus? Rather than preaching personal opinions and sectarian doctrines, we need to emphasize Jesus— who He is, what He did, what He said, and what He expects of us. As the Gaither song puts it, "There's just something about that name."

Many people grow up knowing other religions, or no religion, but they don't know Jesus. And many who have heard *about* Jesus feel just the way Troy used to. They *think* they know Him, but they really don't. They need to learn the facts about His life, recorded in the four Gospels. They need to know about His caring, His mercy, His authority, His dependability. They need "show and tell." They need to meet believers who will both show and tell about their relationship with God's Son.

That's what happened in Bible times. Acts 4:13 gives a wonderful description of this: "When they saw the courage of Peter and John and realized that they were unschooled, ordinary men, they were astonished and they took note that these men had been with Jesus."

That is happening today!

In a world tired of denominational division and debate, it is refreshing to find Christians who simply seek to follow Jesus. Not some earthly organization. Not some worn creed. Not the latest public opinion poll. Not a self-styled prophet. Not even the best evangelist, elder, or editor you can find. Just Jesus.

His will must be obeyed. His words must be our law. What He says goes in the church. "He is the head of the body, the church" (Colossians 1:18). What He says goes in our personal lives, too. "*All* authority in heaven and on earth has been given to me," Jesus said (Matthew 28:18).

We must believe not in some statement about Christ, but *in Christ himself.*

The old song puts it like this:

> What He says we will do,
> Where He sends we will go,
> Never fear, only trust and obey.[2]

Since Jesus returned to Heaven more than 2000 years ago, many of His followers have written down statements of what they believe. These are called "creeds." Sincere believers did this in an attempt to maintain strong faith and to correct heresies. "You must say exactly what we have said about Jesus if you are to be a *true* Christian," they argue. But these creeds have proved divisive. None has established orthodoxy to everyone's satisfaction.

Over the centuries certain religious groups have clustered about certain creeds. In addition to having faith in Jesus as the Son of God, to be a part of that group you must also agree to their creedal statement.

For example, faith in Christ plus the Augsburg Confession makes you a Lutheran.

Faith in Christ plus the Methodist Discipline makes you a Methodist.

Faith in Christ plus the Philadelphia Confession makes you a Baptist.

Faith in Christ plus the Westminster Confession makes you a Presbyterian.

But faith in Christ *alone* makes you simply a Christian.

Isn't that enough?

"The Bible only makes Christians only." Wouldn't it be wonderful if everyone around the world who believes in Jesus could be united to—not separated from—every other believer? Why must Christians be divided into groups, each embracing some human statement of faith?

This is not to suggest that we should be indifferent to what a person believes. Not at all. Peter declared, "You are the Christ, the Son of the living God" (Matthew 16:16). That means something! This statement has been called "the good confession" (1 Timothy 6:13). We must believe not in some statement *about* Christ, but *in Christ himself*. He is the sole foundation for the church (1 Corinthians 3:11).

When a person confesses Christ, false views are excluded. "I believe that Jesus Christ is the Son of the living God." The word *God* excludes atheism; *the* excludes polytheism; *living* excludes pantheism; *Son* excludes unitarianism; and *Christ* excludes gnosticism. There is no doubt left as to what a person means, thinks, and believes when the "good confession" is honestly affirmed.

When a person confesses faith in Jesus, we don't have to ask, "Do you believe the Old Testament?" Jesus said that He came to fulfill all that was written there (Matthew 5:17). We don't have to ask, "Do you believe what the apostles wrote?" Jesus promised that the Holy Spirit would guide them into all truth (John 16:13). We don't have to ask, "Are you willing to be baptized?" Jesus commanded baptism (Matthew 28:18-20). He is King. He is Lord. We believe all that He said and did. He is the one creed that needs no revision—"the same yesterday, today, forever" (Hebrews 13:8).

Think of it this way. If a creed or statement of faith has *more* than the Bible, it has too much. If it has *less* than the Bible, it has too little. If it is exactly *the same* as the Bible, it is unnecessary. Some argue that we must have the clarification and explanation found in a creed. Alexander Campbell responded to this by asking, "Can we improve on God? How can noninspired men speak more intelligently, more definitively, or more clearly than inspired?"

Rubel Shelly put it well:

The . . . reason why I favor the attempt to practice undenominational Christianity is that it is Christ-honoring. Sectarian versions of Christianity are hardly in position to give the glory to Christ which He alone should have. Instead they tend to give honor to human leaders, human opinions, and even human creedal formulations of beliefs rather than simply centering their faith around Christ and the cross![3]

Then he added,

There are important figures of history to whom I am indebted. They have done great things and rendered sacrificial services. but I could never wear their names for the sake of declaring my spiritual allegiance or identification. Whatever those men have done that is of value has served to point others to Christ. Surely that is the mission we have in our generation—not to exalt ourselves, but to lift up Christ.[4]

The church we read about in the New Testament had no creed but Christ himself. When accepting Christ, penitent believers simply affirmed, "I believe that Jesus is the Christ, the Son of the living God" (Acts 8:37). Why should we require something more or different today? Simple trust in Jesus as the Messiah is essential for every Christian.

Moreover, when people follow only Christ, churches will grow.

At the 2002 North American Christian Convention meeting in Columbus, Ohio, Jim Garlow was one of the guest speakers. He preaches for the Skyline Wesleyan Church near San Diego, California. His topic was, "An Outsider's View of the Restoration Movement."

He commended the kind of churches that he called "Jesus-centered." That is exactly what we must seek to be. Wearing only Christ's name, accepting only His authority, we try to follow our Lord in every way. As we do, we must always point everyone to Jesus. It may be easy for people to find fault with the church, but no one can find any fault with Jesus. The closer we are to Christ, the closer we will be to one another.

Garlow commended the Christian Churches and Churches of Christ for turning a corner. You have moved, Garlow observed, "from merely getting people from other churches (as you did in the mid-1800s) to truly evangelizing the lost." He added, "Some of your megachurches are profoundly skilled in doing exactly what the original call of God is: to get the gospel out and present Jesus in such a compelling fashion that people will respond."[5]

When I was growing up in New Mexico, my aunt and uncle lived in a little town in the Texas panhandle. They attended the Methodist Church there. Everyone loved their preacher; the people just called him "Brother Don." When I visited them, I sometimes would hear Brother Don preach.

Once back in the 1950s, he said something like this: "You know, folks, there are some leaders in our denomination who have actually made the statement they think that on some subjects Jesus was mistaken." He paused, then added, "Now I don't know how you folks feel, but as for *me*, I'll take what Jesus said!"

That's what we must tell the world today. As for *us*, we'll take what Jesus said! We must maintain the simple goal of restoring New Testament Christianity. It has never been more relevant. It has never been more needed. We must faithfully follow Jesus and His Word.

As we do, let us resist setting ourselves apart from any other believer. Instead, let us reach out with hands of love to all who acknowledge Jesus as Lord and want to follow Him. Let us teach them, and let us learn from them. Let's all just follow Jesus!

ENDNOTES

1. Franklin Graham, *The Name* (Nashville: Thomas Nelson, 2002) 57.
2. J.H. Sammis, "Trust and Obey." Public domain.
3. Rubel Shelly, *I Just Want to Be a Christian* (Nashville: 20th-Century Christian, 1984) 35.
4. Ibid., 36, 37.
5. Jim Garlow, "An Outsider's View of the Restoration Movement," *Christian Standard*, November 10, 2001, 12. (The entire article is reprinted in the appendix.)

5

FOLLOWING GOD'S WORD

Authority of Scripture.

If we are to follow Jesus, it's only natural that we would follow His Word. After all, it is Scripture that tells us all that we know about Jesus. It's difficult to think of something we know for sure about Christ that is not recorded in the Bible.

Rubel Shelly explains, "Undenominational Christianity honors Christ as the personal embodiment of its faith and acknowledges Holy Scripture as its only propositional formulation. Jesus alone is looked to as Savior; Scripture alone is subscribed to as the basis for our faith in Him."[1]

Many people *say* that they follow God's Word, of course. Not all really do. Jesus warned, "Not everyone who says to me on that day, 'Lord, Lord,' will enter the kingdom of heaven, but only he who does the will of my Father who is in heaven" (Matthew 7:21).

Following God's Word includes active obedience, not just passive assent. "Do not merely listen to the word, and so deceive yourselves. Do what it says" (James 1:22). James then added, "A person is justified by what he *does* and *not by faith alone*" (James 2:24).

We want to encourage all people of every religious background, and all who have no religious background, to recognize and follow the truth of God's Word. It is the final authority for all matters in the church.

TRUST ITS ACCURACY

Some folk *claim* to follow Scripture, but question its accuracy and dependability. "Is it really true? All of it?" Ample evidence is available to convince an honest doubter.[2] Christians have found there is no valid reason to doubt the Bible. On the contrary, there is strong evidence to show that it is indeed the Word of God.

Scripture claims nothing less. The apostle Paul wrote, "All Scripture is God-breathed and is useful for teaching, rebuking, correcting and training in righteousness, so that the man of God may be thoroughly equipped for every good work" (2 Timothy 3:16,17).

At Clovernook Christian Church, Cincinnati, Ohio, a 20-something college student spoke about how he came to believe in the Bible. Chris Travis said,

> About four years ago I was an atheist who thought that the Bible was not true. One day, I stopped and bought a copy of the *King James Version* of the Bible from a little bookstore not far from here. I took it home and began to read it on page one. My plan was to read it straight through like a novel. I was looking for some answers to some pretty big questions— questions about life and existence and meaning. Questions that I hadn't found satisfactory answers to in any of the literature of philosophy I had studied up until that point.
>
> I was thinking something like, "I need to put my money where my mouth is." You see, I had been saying that the Bible wasn't true. But really, that was just something I had heard other people say. I had never investigated it for myself.
>
> As I read the documents that have been collected together to form the Bible, I was just taken aback at how well they seemed to represent the way things really are. And the language was so beautiful; the stories were so original and compelling; the characters were so believable—especially the character and the words of Jesus. When I got into the New Testament and encountered the records of His life and teaching, I was struck by how other-worldly and countercultural His words were. I began to become convinced that human beings alone could not have written words like these, or invented a character like this one. There must have been some kind of higher intelligence involved in their creation. There must be some Higher Being who partnered with these humans to write this book.

Because Chris was honest, he gave the Bible fair consideration. This is all that anyone needs to do. Intellectual honesty requires one to study *all* of the evidence. Some raise questions or cast doubt on the Bible. Don't let them keep you from giving it careful evaluation. Scripture can stand full examination by any honest doubter. As Lynn Deshazo's beautiful chorus says, "*Ancient words ever true, Changing me changing you.*"

God's Word is infallible. We can trust it. We can count on it. We can depend upon its promises, and we should certainly be cautioned by its warnings. An outline often used in Restoration Movement teaching and interpretation of Scripture suggests that the gospel message consists of four elements:

1. Facts to be believed,
2. Commands to be obeyed,
3. Promises to be received,
4. Warnings to be heeded.

It's interesting to use this approach as you study the first gospel sermon (Acts 2). Note that all four elements are included in Luke's inspired report of that dramatic message. On the day of Pentecost, for the first time, the apostles were able to announce the essence of the gospel—the death, burial, and resurrection of Christ (1 Corinthians 15:1-4). On that day, in Jerusalem, about AD 33, the church began. Rooted in Scripture, the church's birth fulfilled all of the relevant Old Testament prophecies.

AFFIRM ITS AUTHORITY

Our Lord's own emphasis on the written Word is quite evident. Jesus declared, "Scripture cannot be broken" (John 10:35). He told His apostles they would be guided into all truth (John 16:13). He prayed specifically, "Sanctify them by the truth. Your word is truth" (John 17:17). Divine inspiration assures the validity of everything in the Bible (2 Peter 1:21).

Later Christ prayed for all who would believe in Him through the message of Scripture. "I pray also for those who will believe in me through their (the apostles) message, that all of them may be one" (John 17:20).

We want to encourage all people of *every* religious background, and all who have *no* religious background, to recognize and follow the truth of God's Word. It is the final authority for all matters in the church.

We must be true to Scripture. Paul told the Philippians, "Stand firm in one spirit, contending as one man for the faith of the gospel" (Philippians 1:27). In the changing winds of modern society, the Bible stands as a solid rock. It is the foundation of the church.

Some seem to think you should just "love everybody" and not make an issue about what the Bible says. Paul had a different view. He told the church in Rome, "Let God be true, and every man a liar" (Romans 3:4). We must bend our will to His.

Isn't it a lot more loving to tell a person *the truth* than to let him believe *a lie*? Real love desires what is best for another. Surely we want people we care about to know what the Bible says about Heaven and Hell. We dare not let our faith be shaped by society, parroting only what is politically

Following God's Word

correct. J.B. Phillips paraphrases Romans 12:2 like this: "Don't let the world around you squeeze you into its own mold, but let God remold your minds from within."

The writer of Hebrews offered his own similar word of caution, and it's still as fresh as this morning's news, "But encourage one another daily, as long as it is called Today, so that none of you may be hardened by sin's deceitfulness" (Hebrews 3:13).

Hearts and minds can be remolded, reshaped, and renewed, especially "Today!" For churches that seek to stand only on the truth of God's Word, this is a wonderful day in the history of the church! What a message we have for the divided religious world!

Today: multiplied thousands of people are seeking out nondenominational churches.

Today: small study groups and large meetings alike are bringing together people from varying religious backgrounds who want simply to study and to follow *only* the Bible.

Today: thousands of Roman Catholics are questioning a church which can have massive changes in practice in areas where they once demanded unquestioning obedience.

Today: thousands of mainline Protestants, disenchanted with the social-political tirades of radical theologians, are looking for those who still hold the basic tenets of historic Christendom.

Today: we "simple Christians" have the right message—"Follow God's Word!"

We have a slogan, "The Bible only makes Christians only." We seek to restore the ideal of the church as it is described in the New Testament. Scripture is our all-sufficient rule of faith and practice for everything in the church (2 Timothy 3:16,17).

Another slogan used by early leaders in this movement goes, "Where the Scripture speaks, we speak. Where the Scripture is silent, we are silent." They meant this: on any topic where the Bible has spoken, the issue is settled for us. There is no debate. We must affirm and practice all that God's Word says. But on the myriad of topics where Scripture offers no specific direction, each person is free to follow what he or she considers the wisest course. On such matters, we are silent, allowing others to hold *their* opinions, not insisting they share *ours*. While we are generous on all nonessential issues, we remain unyielding on any subject where we find a "Thus saith the Lord."

INTERPRET IT CORRECTLY

All men and women can come to the Bible on their own. They need no priest, no pastor, no professor, no preacher to stand between them and God's Word. Everyone can study it without an intermediary. Then they can reach their own conclusions, in light of what *they* find in Scripture. This is at the heart of nonsectarian Christianity.

While we hold Scripture alone as the basis for what we do and say in the church, we realize that every Bible verse isn't understood in the same way by every person who reads it.

A student once asked a Bible college professor, "How should you interpret the Scripture—literally or figuratively?"

He replied, "Neither. You should interpret it intelligently!"

. . . we *must* all affirm that whatever the Bible says is both accurate and authoritative. Then we must do our best to understand and obey it.

That's easier said than done, of course. Some texts are obviously figurative. Others definitely aren't. Still others seem to fall somewhere in between. On such texts sincere, Bible-believing students may come to different conclusions. We don't have to agree with each other on every interpretation of every Bible verse, but we *must* all affirm that whatever the Bible says is both accurate and authoritative. Then we must do our best to understand and obey it.

A student should ask three simple questions of any Bible text: 1) Who is speaking? 2) To whom? 3) What are the circumstances? In the appendix helpful resources are listed to help one interpret the Bible accurately. This field of study is called Hermeneutics. (See bibliography.)

More than 40 years ago Professor R.C. Foster wrote in the *Standard Lesson Commentary:*

All of us need to study the New Testament and bring our faith and practice into harmony with it. No human being can claim a copyright on all truth. We must always be ready to hold the Scriptures, and not ourselves, as the divine pattern. The proposition of restoring the church as seen in the New Testament resolves itself into these declarations: If anything that I believe or practice is not in accord with the New Testament, then I desire to discover it and abandon it. If anything the New Testament teaches is missing from my belief or practice, then I want to include it. Speak, Lord, for thy servant heareth.[3]

Apply It Faithfully

Some of the truths commonly accepted and understood by members of Christian Churches and Churches of Christ today were not so evident to the early leaders in this movement. Many of them had grown up in the Presbyterian Church.

At one meeting in 1809 in rural Pennsylvania, Thomas Campbell affirmed the principle, "Where the Scripture speaks, we speak. Where the Scripture is silent, we are silent." One of the men present, Andrew Munro, said, "Mr. Campbell, if we adopt *that* as a basis, then there is an end of infant baptism." Campbell didn't think that it would be, but he did believe the principle was valid regardless. So he replied, "Of course, if infant baptism be not found in Scripture, we can have nothing to do with it."[4] Later, when he did not find it in the Bible, he gave up the practice.

Since that time a host of other Bible students have changed *their* view of baptism also. They tried to study honestly what the Bible says, then apply it faithfully in their lives. Scripture must be our guide, wherever it may lead us.

This premise is still valid. I remember the liberating sense of freedom I received in a class taught by Professor Woodrow Phillips at Ozark Christian College many years ago. He said, "Suppose I find some church down the street practicing something that we have not been doing, but that the Bible clearly commands. If that happened, I would not leave the Christian Church and go join *that* congregation. I would stay where I am and just start practicing the new truth I had learned from God's Word."

That's it in a nutshell.

We must always remain open to *every* truth in the Bible. Such a commitment is comfortable. It is honest. It is fair and realistic. None of us are perfect, but God's Word is. We do not want to perpetuate any sectarian teaching by *anyone*—including leaders of the Restoration Movement (such as Barton Stone or Alexander Campbell). We strive to follow only the Bible, not *any* human being.

Years ago Barton W. Stone was studying to be a Presbyterian minister. He lived in Kentucky in 1798. Stone believed firmly in the Bible as the authoritative Word of God, but he had doubts about man-made documents that were important to his church, such as the Westminster Confession of Faith. He was not sure about the doctrines of election and predestination as they were taught there. He described his feelings in his autobiography:

In this state of mind, the day appointed for my ordination found me. I had determined to tell the Presbytery honestly the state of my mind, and to request them to defer my ordination until I should be better informed and settled. The Presbytery came together, and a large congregation attended. Before its constitution, I took aside the two pillars of it, Doct. James Blythe and Robert Marshall, and made known to them my difficulties. . . . They labored, but in vain, to remove my difficulties and objections. They asked me how far I was willing to receive the confession? I told them, as far as I saw it consistent with the word of God. They concluded that was sufficient.

I went into the Presbytery, and when the question was proposed, "Do you receive and adopt the Confession of Faith, as containing the system of doctrine taught in the Bible?" I answered aloud, so that the whole congregation might hear, "I do, as far as I see it consistent with the word of God." No objection being made, I was ordained.[5]

The Word of God was Barton Stone's supreme authority, and it must be ours as well. We need follow no manmade traditions, only the truth of Scripture.

ENDNOTES

1. Shelly, *I Just Want*, 40.
2. Those wanting resources on the accuracy of the Bible might find these helpful:
   Lee Strobel, *The Case for Christ* (Grand Rapids: Zondervan, 1998).
   Lynn Gardner, *Christianity Stands True* (Joplin, MO: College Press, 1994).
     Popular studies on hermeneutics (the interpretation of Scripture) include:
   Gordon D. Fee and Douglas Steward, *How to Read the Bible for All Its Worth* (Grand Rapids: Zondervan, 1993).
   J. Scott Duvall and Danny Hays, *Grasping God's Word* (Grand Rapids: Zondervan; Ouachita Baptist University, 2001).
   Robert Palmer, *How to Understand the Bible* (Joplin, MO: College Press, 1980)
3. R.C. Foster, *Standard Lesson Commentary*, Standard Publishing (*Bible Teacher and Leader*, March 19, 1960).
4. Robert Richardson, *Memoirs of Alexander Campbell* (Nashville: Gospel Advocate, 1956, reprint ed.) 238.
5. Barton W. Stone. *A Short History of the Life of Barton W. Stone*, written by himself. Reprinted in *Voices from Cane Ridge* (St. Louis: Bethany Press, 1954) 59, 60.

6

FAITH, FREEDOM, AND LOVE

Charles M. Schulz, creator of the legendary *Peanuts* cartoon strip, has also drawn a series of cartoons featuring teenagers. In one of them he shows an enthusiastic young man speaking to a group of friends. He says, "I take my religion seriously! I get into arguments almost every day!"

People often argue about the Bible. But many of the differences between Christians are not so much over what Scripture actually *says*, but about *their opinions about what it says.*

This is nothing new. Back in the 1800s, for example, believers were divided over such matters as who would be permitted to take Communion, who should be baptized and how, and what names were appropriate for a believer to wear. A number of Christian leaders from different denominations decided it was time to do something.

They knew division was wrong, and they wanted to find a biblical basis for unity. Rather than arguing about issues that didn't matter, they determined to see what did. Then they determined to do something about it. They liked a statement made centuries before by Rupertus Meldinius. He said, "In essentials, we must have unity. In non-essentials, let us allow liberty. And in all things, let us show love." They decided to pray and work and study and act together in an effort—a movement—to restore, in every way possible, the original practices and principles of early church Christianity.

Such an approach provided then, and still provides today, a way for believers from every Christian background to lay aside sectarian, denominational teachings and hold simply to the original message and methods of the church pictured in the New Testament. A person seeking pure water in a polluted stream follows it back to where it originates. A stream is always purest at its source. So it is with the church. We need to see what the church was like when it began.

It is clear that Christ established only one church, not hundreds of competing denominations (Matthew 16:18). It is also evident that He wanted His followers to be united, not divided (John 17:20,21). The intent of the Restoration Movement is for all the Lord's followers to stand together in matters of faith, to allow freedom in matters of opinion, and to show love to all in the process.

WHAT ARE MATTERS OF FAITH?

Obviously some elements of Christianity are essential—valid for every time and place. But how can we know which they are?

Why not determine the essentials by the specific statements of Scripture itself? Isn't that a safe basis? If the New Testament says that something is a certain way, it is. We can, and must, follow God's Word.

An opinion, on the other hand, is an inference deduced from Scripture. Here we may differ. While we must believe what *the Bible* says about a topic, we don't have to share the same *opinion* about what the Bible says. Unless something is specifically stated in the Bible, no one has the right or authority to insist that anyone agree with what he or she thinks on the subject.

Thomas Campbell was one of the pioneers of the Restoration Movement. Back in 1809 he authored what Dr. James North has called "probably the most significant document that the Restoration Movement has produced"—the Declaration and Address.[1] Campbell included thirteen propositions intended to discover the principles by which the church could be united.

In Proposition VI, Thomas Campbell affirmed:

Although inferences and deductions from Scripture premises, when fairly inferred, may be truly called the doctrine of God's holy word, yet are they not formally binding upon the consciences of Christians farther than they perceive the connection. . . . No such deductions can be made terms of communion, but do properly belong to the after and progressive edification of the church."[2]

North observes, "This idea is dynamite! Campbell is saying: Be sure to make a distinction between what Scripture says and what you think it means. Logical deductions are human conclusions, and they are not to be confused with the teaching of Scripture itself."[3]

It's like this. Suppose a serviceman is ordered to report to a certain military base at a certain time on a certain day in preparation for deploy-

Faith, Freedom, and Love

ment overseas. His order doesn't specify how he is to get there. He might take a train, a plane, a bus, a car, a horse, or a motorcycle. He could even hitchhike! He is responsible to obey the order—but beyond that, he is allowed freedom to choose the details of *how* to obey it. No officer can demand that the soldier use that CO's preferred method of transportation in order to reach the base. It is much the same for the church.

For example, Scripture directs Christians to worship. It doesn't tell them that they have to meet in a church building, however. In fact, there may not have been any church buildings as such until the third century A.D. If you look carefully through the pages of the New Testament, you will find that the first Christians met in different places—an upper room (Acts 1:13), by a river (Acts 16:13ff), and in a house (Philemon 2). Obviously the place where we meet is not important to the Lord, though He *does* care about what we do *when* we worship (see John 4:24).

Sometimes the churches met on Saturday night (the Sabbath). One service that started then went on until midnight! (Acts 20:7). (And you thought *your* preacher was long-winded!) The earliest believers met regularly (Acts 2:42). Normally, the Christians met on the first day of the week (Sunday) to "break bread" (Acts 20:7), bring their offerings (1 Corinthians 16:2), sing, and hear messages from the Lord (1 Corinthians 14:26).

Some critics are caustic in their responses to those of us who seek to restore the church as seen in the pages of the New Testament. "Which church do you want to restore?" they laugh. "Do you want to restore Corinth with its sin? Jerusalem with its prejudice? Which one?"

The answer, of course, is that we do not want to restore the church of Corinth *or* the church of Jerusalem, but the church of Christ. Where the Christians in any city did what was right, we can follow them. Where they were wrong, the inspired account corrects them, and we can choose to follow the biblical way.

When a new car rolls from the assembly line and passes its final inspection, it should be in A-1 condition. So we can expect the church to be most like what the Lord wants it to be immediately after its birth. The New Testament shows us the ideal for the church, both for the individual congregation and for the church universal.

William E. Sweeney, a minister in the early 1900s, used to point out graphically that the essentials of New Testament Christianity have not been altogether lost. They have been the common property of the church universal up to today, he explained. But they are like the paintings on the walls of ancient cathedrals. They have been covered with dust, cobwebs, and debris. To see a painting in its beauty, one must remove what covers it so that what is beneath is made visible to all. In a similar way, the essentials of the church have often been clouded by human opinion and tradition. In both cases, the original form must be restored if we are to see either the painting or the church in its true glory.

So how do we determine what is essential? We turn to the Bible. *OT ?*
Believers from most denominational backgrounds affirm that it is God's Word. *NT ?*
Why not take this approach: "Where the Scripture speaks, we speak. Where *Cultural ?*
the Scripture is silent, we are silent." In matters of faith, where the Bible has *Universal ?*
spoken, there we must stand together united. But this does not mean that we have to see eye-to-eye on every opinion.

WHAT ARE MATTERS OF OPINION?

Many debates among religious people today are about things where the Bible gives no specific "Thus saith the Lord." In such cases, individuals have the right to their own opinions and preferences.

Take baptism, for example.

The Scripture clearly shows that Christ commanded all believers to be baptized (Matthew 28:18-20). He promised salvation, forgiveness, and the gift of the Holy Spirit to those repentant disciples who are baptized (Mark 16:16; Acts 2:38). Baptism is a burial in water (Romans 6:3-6). When one is baptized, he or she is not baptized into a local congregation, but into union with Christ himself (Romans 6:5). People are to be baptized "in the name of the Father, and of the Son, and of the Holy Spirit" (Matthew 28:19).

These points are obviously, unequivocally taught in God's Word.

But what about *who* is to do the baptizing?

Or *when* it is to be done?

Or *where* it is to be done?

Or *what clothing* one should wear for the event?

Or *what other words could be said* (besides those in Matthew 28:19)?

Or *how old* a child must be before being baptized?

On these questions, and many more like them, there is no biblical mandate. One of my Bible college professors used to say that in such cases, we should apply "sanctified common sense." Since then, I have found that common sense isn't all that common! What seems so obvious and clear to me isn't always seen that way by others!

For example, someone might insist upon immersing believers in *running* water. That's OK. I don't think it *has* to be that way, but that can be your choice. (As a matter of fact, when I first baptized someone almost 50 years ago, it *was* in a stream.) Normally, I prefer a baptistery though.

Such things are matters of opinion.

The New Testament itself is replete with examples of similar liberty in methods of evangelism. Matthew 28:18-20 instructs us to preach the gospel, baptize believers, and then disciple them, but it leaves the details of how we do it up to us.

The earliest Christians had different opinions at times, but they were united on the essential mission of the church. What's more, they treated each other with love. (This aspect of the New Testament church will be treated more fully in chapter 6.)

Church history demonstrates the reasonableness and value of allowing freedom and flexibility in anything that is not a matter of faith. When it comes to what a person must do to be saved, we want to stand simply on what the Bible plainly states. We call for people to believe that Jesus is the Christ, the Son of the living God. This is the basis of our faith. It was the central conviction of those first-century converts to Christianity as well. Affirming faith in Christ was filled with meaning (Romans 10:9). Every Bible-believing religious group agrees with the essential nature of faith in Jesus as a fundamental aspect of salvation through and relationship with Him.

We encourage believers to make a public confession of belief in Christ, and this also meets with general approval. We insist on repentance—turning *toward* God and *away from* sin—and so do all. We immerse in water those who have done these things.

Evangelists, preachers, pastors, and scholars of every distinct denomination (including leaders of the Roman Catholic or Greek Orthodox churches) agree about the validity and significance of immersion as an aspect of biblical practice and faith. All agree that such baptism is appropriate. It fits with Scripture and with church history. The immersion of a believer in the name of the Father, Son, and Holy Spirit is accepted by those of any sect of Christianity—regardless of the method their church may normally practice. Jesus himself was baptized, that is, immersed.. Why change it? There is "one Lord, one faith, one baptism" (Ephesians 4:5)

How Do We Put It into Practice?

The New Testament offers some beautiful examples of flexibility practiced by the first-century church. Scripture encourages Christians to show understanding and grace in dealing with brothers and sisters—especially when they are coming from different backgrounds.

This is illustrated in Romans 14. The church at Rome had in its membership some who came from a Jewish background. Others were Gentiles. The two groups were completely different in their culture and upbringing. Apparently some Jewish Christians were not willing to give up certain requirements of the Old Testament law (such as dietary restrictions or Sabbath observances). Most Gentile Christians didn't hold themselves accountable to these traditions.

Paul counseled them carefully in Romans 14:1-3:

Accept him whose faith is weak, without passing judgment on disputable matters. One man's faith allows him to eat everything, but another man, whose faith is weak, eats only vegetables. The man who eats everything must not look down on him who does not, and the man who does not eat everything must not condemn the man who does, for God has accepted him.

Christians don't have to agree on such "disputable matters." Further, when we *do* disagree, we should not pass judgment on each other, condemning someone because he doesn't share our opinion or preference. "Who are you to judge someone else's servant?" Paul asked (Romans 14:4). "To his own master he stands or falls. And he will stand, for the Lord is able to make him stand."

The apostle went ever further. "We who are strong ought to bear with the failings of the weak and not to please ourselves. Each of us should please his neighbor for his good, to build him up. For even Christ did not please himself" (Romans 15:1-3).

We *can* allow a brother to hold his opinion, but we *cannot* allow him to make that opinion a test of fellowship. Neither can we insist that *our* opinion must be law for *him*. Everything is to be done in a spirit of love and humility.

In addition to differences we may have in applying Scripture, at times we will also have differences in personal evaluation and matters of judgment. Such cases call for a similar response. The experience of Paul and Barnabas (Acts 15:37-40) is filled with lessons for us on this subject.

Paul and Barnabas disagreed about whom to take with them on a missionary trip. Barnabas thought John Mark should join them; Paul didn't. This was not a matter of right or wrong. It was a matter of personal judgment. When their differences seemed irreconcilable, Barnabas took Mark and Paul took Silas. Then both teams went off to evangelize and encourage. Note that they did not bad-mouth each other, criticize each other, or condemn each other. They simply agreed to disagree, and they continued to serve the Lord, though they did it separately. Everyone was comfortable with the decision.

We can learn several things from their experience:

1. Devout Christians can and will disagree at times.

2. It is OK to work separately if two cannot work together harmoniously.

3. In such cases, it is not necessary to criticize or condemn the other person.

4. When a nonjudgmental spirit is shown, the work can continue to be blessed. After Paul and Barnabas separated, *two* teams went out instead of just one!

As a postscript, it is interesting to note that, later on, Paul worked alongside Mark again (Colossians 4:10).

In churches today, preferences in the type of worship service and music style often become divisive. Some people are concerned about using an overhead projector rather than a hymnal, singing praise choruses instead of hymns, standing instead of sitting, following a worship team instead of a song leader. The grievance list can go on and on.

It is understandable that we each have our preferences, but there is no need to allow these differences to become unity-threatening issues. We each have in mind what is the best kind of worship service. That's fine. But we need to ask, "Where did we get this idea?" Usually we like what is comfortable and familiar to us. Our choices are based not so much on Scripture as from our experiences and our culture.

Why can't we permit variety in methods? If I love my neighbors as myself, can't I learn to worship sometimes in a way *they* enjoy? Instead of being bored by that slow, old hymn tune, can't I focus on the message and sing it sincerely because it is good, because it serves as a reminder of great spiritual truths? Instead of being irritated by the throb of drums, can't I join happily in that lively chorus because honoring the command to "sing to the Lord a new song" (Psalm 96:1 et al.) pleases God?

When the apostle Paul faced similar questions regarding matters of opinion, not matters of faith, he was as broadminded as could be (see 1 Corinthians 9:19-23). He declared, "I have become all things to all men so that by all possible means I might save some" (v. 22). We must stand solidly on biblical faith, yet allow freedom in matters of opinion. We each can have our opinion; others can have theirs. And in all things, *all* of us must show love. When this happens, differences need not divide.

ENDNOTES

1. Thomas Campbell, *Declaration and Address* (Lincoln, Ill: College and Seminary Press, n.d.). Quoted by James B. North, *Union in Truth.*

2. North, *Union*, 90.

3. Ibid.

7

UNITY IN CHRIST

<Christians need to stand together in their battle against the devil, not fight each other. It's like the young boy who had been getting in trouble all afternoon. His exasperated mother finally told him, "I'm getting my belt, and you're going to get a spanking!" The little fellow took off running up the stairs.

About that time his dad came home. "What's the matter?" he asked his wife. "It's that son of yours," she said. Then she told him what all had happened. "I'll take care of it," the father assured her. He went upstairs looking for the boy. He couldn't find him anywhere. Finally he went into the boy's room and heard him underneath the bed. His dad got down on his knees, and started to crawl under the bed after him. The little guy said, "Is she after you, too?"

". . . what we have in common is so much more important than what separates us."

A DESIRABLE GOAL

Sometimes we forget who the enemy is. It's not other Christians. Not each other. We are to fight the devil and his forces. To do that, the church must act as one. No wonder our Lord prayed on the night of His betrayal, "I pray also for those who will believe in me through their [the apostles'] message, that all of them may be one, Father, just as you are in me and I am in you" (John 17:20,21).

Jesus cared about the unity of His people. We must as well.

The apostle Paul also emphasized unity. "Make every effort to keep the unity of the Spirit through the bond of peace" (Ephesians 4:3). The Jews and Gentiles who made up the church in Ephesus had been at enmity with each other for years. Now they were one in Christ! "Keep the unity," Paul directed. The unity of the Spirit isn't something men create; it is given by God. Our responsibility is to maintain it, to guard it, to preserve it.

David Lipscomb put it this way: "The spirit that promotes unity and harmony among men comes from God. Unity and harmony of action are impossible in a way not provided by God. That unity is gained and maintained by doing the will of God. It requires no negotiations or arrangements among men to unite them as one in Christ. If we are in Christ, we cannot help being one with all who are in Christ."[1]

This unity *did* exist in the first-century church. Look at Acts 4:32: "All the believers were one in heart and mind." That is unity in Christ. The believers were all following the one Spirit-inspired message. When men and women follow that same message today, the same unity can exist.

We need to do all that is within our power to help. Popular speaker and writer Max Lucado spoke on this topic at a national gathering of ministers from many religious groups. It was at a "Clergy Summit" sponsored by Promise Keepers. He pointed out John 13:35: "All people will know that you are my followers if you love each other." Then he asked, "Could it be that *unity* is the key to reaching the world for Christ? If unity is the key to evangelism, shouldn't it have precedence in our prayers?"[2]

He went on, "If unity matters to God, then shouldn't unity matter to us? If unity is a priority in heaven, then shouldn't it be a priority on earth?"

To maintain unity with others should not be so difficult. In fact, Lucado observed, "It should be simple. Where there is faith, repentance, and a new birth, there is a Christian. When I meet a man whose faith is in the cross and whose eyes are on the Savior, I meet a brother."[3]

The apostle Paul told the Christians in Philippi, "Stand firm in one Spirit, contending as one man for the faith of the gospel" (Philippians 1:27). If we're honest, we have to admit that Christians today are often a long way from demonstrating the unity for which Christ prayed and for which Paul pleaded.

It's a little like the preacher who decided to find out if the people in his church really loved him. Brother Smith decided on a devious method to try to find out. He slipped over to the church building late one Sunday afternoon and tacked a sign on the door. It said, "Brother Smith departed for Heaven—4:00 p.m."

Then he hid in the bushes nearby to watch the reactions of those coming for the Sunday evening service. He wanted to find out which members were sad at his demise. After about an hour someone walked up, read the note, wrote something on the paper, then turned and walked away.

This was too much for the preacher. His curiosity got the best of him. He slipped out from behind the shrubbery, and hurried over by the door. The note was still the same at the top: "Brother Smith departed for Heaven—4:00 p.m." But below that were scrawled the words, "P.S. Heaven—5:00 p.m. Brother Smith has not arrived *here* yet!"

This is a picture of the church today. Divided and subdivided Christianity has not yet arrived at the heavenly station. Even in the Restoration Movement, the ideal of a united, universal church has not always been maintained. People have moved to the right and to the left. Some have put self above the Savior. But God's ideal for the church remains unchanged in His Word!

One of the most common excuses non-Christians give for not going to church is, "Which church should I attend? You say yours is right, and my friend down the street says hers is right. How can I know what to believe?"

To that person we would say, "We don't ask you to follow our church. We just ask you to follow the Bible. Read for yourself what it teaches, and then do what it says." You can't go wrong just following God's Word. You need no denominational headquarters, no synod, no presbytery, no conference, no hierarchy to tell you what to do.

A WORKABLE PLAN

We can listen to what a lot of different people say, but we must test what *any* church leader says by the words of Scripture. This makes sense to many believers in today's world. To them we say, "Why not work with us as we seek to bring about the unity of the church?"

Some years ago I studied at Earlham College, Richmond, Indiana. The school is operated by the Society of Friends. One class was a graduate course in Christian Education. Six students were enrolled. Each was from a different religious group. Of course, the professor was a Quaker. One day we were each telling about our church background. I said that I was from the Christian Church. A lady from the United Brethren Church asked the professor, "What does the Christian Church believe?"

He had studied at Butler University, and knew something about the Restoration Movement. He began by saying, "They believe that denominationalism is wrong. They feel that Christians shouldn't be divided. They don't want to wear any human names. They try to follow the church in the Bible, and depend largely upon the book of Acts, and they feel there is just one church."

The lady said, "Oh, and they think that *they* are . . ."

I interrupted her. "Just a minute," I explained. "We have a saying, 'We are not the only Christians, but we are Christians only." The professor affirmed that this indeed was our position.

In this movement to restore the church to the order, faith, and life of the church pictured in the New Testament, we have never said, "Only those in our group are Christians." Our understanding is that any time a person obeys the requirements of Christ to be saved, God adds that person to the church, and he or she is therefore a Christian (Acts 2:47). Obviously there are many in different religious groups who have done that. For this reason we gladly welcome into the membership of our churches other penitent, immersed believers who want to unite with us. Together we would follow only Jesus, obey only His Word.

Our question is, "Why can't we *all* just be *Christians*? Why should we set ourselves apart from other believers? Why can't we all wear only Christ's name?" We don't *want* to be another denomination. We don't *intend* to be one. Why should a person have to say, "I'm this kind of a Christian or that kind"? Why can't all of us lay aside *all* of our labels? Why can't we just take God's Word as our sole authority, and simply wear the name of our Savior?

A special issue of *The Lookout* magazine had as its theme, "Simply Christian," and we have chosen it for the title of this book.[4] Simply Christian! That says it all. That is what we want to be. In this way, we hope to encourage the unity of all God's people.

A few years ago I saw a television documentary describing the commitment of the Zionist element in Israel. The film showed thousands of Jews returning to their ancestral land. They came from all over the world. Different languages. Different clothes. Different food. Acknowledging these differences, one Israeli explained, "We have found that what we have in common is so much more important than what separates us."

What a lesson for those who wear Christ's name! Divided by opinions, traditions, and culture, we also have something far more important in common—we belong to Jesus! In this spirit, we must reach out in love to the many sincere believers around us. We don't have to agree on every interpretation of Scripture to share in fellowship and faith. We must make the Lord's desire for unity our own. In doing so, we can help answer His prayer in John 17.

This is a plan that works. That fact was illustrated beautifully several years ago by Ziden Nutt, executive director of Good News Productions, International (Joplin, Missouri). He told of the providence surrounding events in late 1976 when Christian leaders from 37 major denominations banded together in a unified effort to use Applied Technology Satellite No. 6 to present the gospel.

The challenge had come through Colonel Lawson Wynne, representing the U.S. Government and NASA. The government would allow the churches to use the experimental communication satellite to present the Christian message, if three conditions were met. All programming had to be: (1) nonsectarian (Bible only, like Frank Borman's reading the Bible on Apollo 10 on Christmas Eve); (2) in the language and culture of the people to whom the programs were beamed; and (3) with no blatant preaching.

On January 9-10, 1981, those churches decreed, "All Christian programs must be presented as depicted and practiced in the first century, according to God's holy Word, the Bible." When this happened, one man turned to Ziden and said, "The message of Ziden's group is tailor-made for this, because all they use is the Bible anyway." This is how the Christian Churches were subsequently asked to head up all of the religious programs for the satellite project!

One gentleman told Ziden afterward, "When I think of how divided the denominations are, and yet how we've all agreed here on just doing things the Bible way, I wonder why we ever chose through the centuries to do things differently."

Christians need to get serious about unity. When Paul wrote the church in Corinth, he told them, "I appeal to you, brothers, in the name of our Lord Jesus Christ, that all of you agree with one another so that there may be no divisions among you and that you may be perfectly united in mind and thought" (1 Corinthians 1:10).

He next told them that he had heard about "quarrels" among them. Some were lining up behind one personality or another. They were creating denominations, in a sense—naming themselves for the person whose "side" they were on. Paul asked them three questions (1 Corinthians 1:13). The same three questions test our loyalties today:

1. Has Christ been divided?
2. Was Paul crucified for you?
3. Were you baptized in the name of Paul?

The obvious answer to each question is "No." Therefore, since no man deserves the loyalty that we owe Jesus, we must sacrifice all personal ambition and desire for position in an effort to exalt Him.

A Beneficial Result

Jesus desires a union that is personal, spiritual, and visible. Seth Wilson, professor emeritus of Ozark Christian College, declared,

> The unity for which Christ prayed is not just any kind of union, but a specified kind and on a specified basis. It is to be personal, every individual united. It is to be spiritual, a harmony of mind, heart, and soul, and not enforced from without. It is to be visible, so that the world will be strongly influenced to believe because of it. Jesus desires the personal unity of each Christian with every other Christian. Such unity can be achieved only as each believer makes Christ the center of his faith and the authority for his life and religious matters.[5]

A lady once took a boat ride on Lake Michigan. It was a stormy night. She watched the jagged lightning streak across the sky, heard the thunder clap, and saw the hazardous rocks jutting out of the wind-tossed lake. She got scared. Going to the captain of the boat she asked, "Do you know where all the rocks are in this lake?"

"No, lady, I don't," he replied, "but I do know the safe course."

I don't know how far a person might drift from the plain teaching in God's Word and still go to Heaven—but I do know the safe course! You can't go wrong to do just what the Bible says. I want to follow His teachings as nearly as I can. Don't you?

ENDNOTES

1. David Lipscomb, *Commentary on Ephesians* (Nashville: Gospel Advocate, 1943) 71.
2. Max Lucado, *In the Grip of Grace* (Dallas: Word. 1996) 163, 164.
3. Ibid., 169.
4. Copies of this special edition are available from *The Lookout*, Standard Publishing, 8121 Hamilton Ave., Cincinnati, OH 45231.
5. Seth Wilson, *Learning from Jesus* (Joplin, MO: College Press, 1977) 414.

8

EVANGELISM

North Star Christian Church is a new congregation planted by the Chicago District Evangelizing Association. Ronnie Cordrey is lead evangelist in this exciting project. "A few months ago," Ronnie explained, "I was talking with a new attendee, Mario. In the late '80s, Mario was heavily involved in a rock band and even had one of his videos debut on MTV. But his life more recently had been filled with problems. A few months ago Mario accepted an invitation from a friend to visit North Star."

"Mario's had a rough past," Ronnie added. "He was married with six kids, when his wife decided to live a lesbian lifestyle. Mario found his world crumbling and falling apart. Mario looked me straight in the eyes and said, 'My heart is broken, my marriage is on the rocks, but ever since I've started coming to North Star, I've found hope and joy through Jesus.'"

He was baptized into Christ on July 20, 2003. He chose that date for a special reason—it's his birthday! He said, "I was born on July 20th, but today I was born into Christ." In recounting the incident, Ronnie concluded, "Never underestimate the power of inviting people to come to church. Never! The power of a changed life is awesome!"

This true story describes what reaching the lost with the gospel really means. Those committed to the restoration of New Testament Christianity are seriously concerned about Christian unity, as we pointed out in the last chapter. But that's not all. Our interest is not unity for the sake of unity, but unity for the sake of world evangelism. We want to help fulfill the prayer of our Lord.

Jesus said, "My prayer is not for them alone. I pray also for those who will believe in me through their message, that all of them may be one, Father, just as you are in me and I am in you. May they also be in us so that the world may believe that you have sent me" (John 17:20,21). He added, "May they be brought to complete unity to let the world know that you sent me and have loved them, even as you have loved me" (v. 23).

Someone put it like this: "The world cannot be won until the church is one." Perhaps the greatest price we are paying for a divided church is an unbelieving world. If every group of Christians around the world were in perfect fellowship and harmony, our job would still not be finished. It would just be started. Bringing the world to faith in Christ is the "Great Commission" Jesus left us (Matthew 28:18-20).

The word "evangelism" comes from the Greek word, *euangelos*, which means "good news." It denotes the same idea as the word "gospel." The apostle Paul declared, "I am not ashamed of the gospel, because it is the power of God for the salvation of everyone who believes" (Romans 1:16). Evangelism is at the heart of the New Testament church. Today some churches have a missionary society. That may be well and good, but the church itself should be seen as a missionary society. Every Christian should be involved in world evangelism with prayer, finances, and encouragement.

PERSONAL RESPONSIBILITY

In the book of Acts the early Christians took seriously the command to evangelize. They did it naturally. It was a part of daily life. When persecution came on the young church, believers were dispersed across the region. "Those who had been scattered preached the word wherever they went," Luke explained (Acts 8:4). These Christians were not silenced by persecution; they were fearless in telling of their faith in the Lord Jesus.

Some Bible scholars suggest that the Great Commission is best understood not as a command ("Go into all the world and preach the gospel"). Rather it could better be translated, "As you are going, preach the gospel." We don't all have to hop on the next plane to Africa to evangelize the world. Wherever we are, we must talk to the people we see each day—coworkers, family, friends. As we go, here or abroad, we can help bring others to our Lord.

Acts 8 contains an example of one Christian's efforts to share his faith. A believer named Philip was on the desert road between Jerusalem and Gaza (Acts 8:26). "He met an Ethiopian eunuch, an important official in charge of all the treasury of Candace, queen of the Ethiopians" (v. 27). The nobleman was reading from the book of Isaiah. Philip asked, "Do you understand what you are reading?"

The man acknowledged his need for help, and invited Philip to ride along with him in his chariot. Luke explains that the man was reading Isaiah 53:7,8. "Philip began with that very passage of Scripture and told him the good news about Jesus" (v. 35). As they traveled, they came to some water and the man said, "Look, here is water. Why shouldn't I be baptized?" Philip agreed. They stopped the chariot, Philip immersed the nobleman, and the new convert "went on his way rejoicing" (v. 39).

This teaches us several important lessons about evangelism in the New Testament Church:

➤ The fact that Philip was not an ordained minister shows that any Christian can baptize.

➤ The fact that it was in the wilderness (no city nearby; certainly no church) shows that baptism is not into a local church as such, but into Christ and His body, the universal church composed of all obedient believers.

➤ The fact that the new convert was a black man demonstrates that the gospel is for men of all races and lands. The gospel is for all the people of every ethnic group, every people group, every language on the earth.

Every Christian should be able to tell someone who Jesus is, what Jesus did, and what that person needs to do to find salvation in Jesus. At the very least, each believer should be able to explain how he or she became a Christian. If we share our faith in a winsome, gracious way, God will bless our efforts. We are not responsible for the results as we witness for Jesus, only that we are found faithful in doing so. The apostle Paul said, "I planted the seed, Apollos watered it, but God made it grow" (1 Corinthians 3:5).

We are not salespeople out to make a pitch, but we are more like farmers out to sow seed (Matthew 13). We take the seed—the Word of God—and sow it. We do that as we tell others about Jesus. Some will be receptive. Others won't. We are not responsible for their decision, only for our obedience. Our responsibility is simply to share our faith.

George Barna has reported that nearly 50 million "born-again" adults—some 60 percent of that population group—shared their faith in Jesus Christ with nonbelievers during the past year.[1] Those doing the best job in sharing their faith are those who believe the Bible is totally accurate in all of its teaching (77 percent of evangelizers questioned said so as compared to 57 percent of those who don't evangelize.) Nondenominational Christian churches made a strong showing, according to the report.

Barna added, "Non-believers are seeking evidence that Christianity is truly life-transforming. Naturally none of us, no matter how committed we are to Christ, will live a perfect life, but the research encourages believers to allow God to change us from the inside out so that our lives will substantiate the difference that following Christ makes."[2]

Christians today are finding various ways in which to reach others for the Master. New church planting has proved to be one of the most effective. Statistics indicate that more unchurched people are willing to visit a new church than an established one. Even in the parts of America with the most congregations, more churches are small and weak than are active, growing, and strong. Even in what might be considered the more religious communities, new churches could and should be started. When this is done, the Lord's kingdom grows more rapidly.

VARIOUS METHODS

Methodology for evangelism has changed over the years. In the earliest days of the Restoration Movement, one group of methods proved effective.[3] Over the past 100 years, things have changed.

Many of the ways in which New Testament Christianity was presented earlier are still being used effectively (e.g., church services, colleges, books, and personal evangelism). But in addition, a great many new ways to communicate faith have been attempted. Many have been successful.[4]

Just what the future holds remains to be seen. We can learn from the past, however. The potential of technology continues to expand. Basic New Testament Christianity is increasingly welcomed by those in many religious groups, as well as those who claim no denominational affiliation. As we seek to evangelize a lost world, we need to remember three don'ts:

1. Don't abandon what is effective.

Some think that if an idea has been around for a while, it's "old hat." Not necessarily. While some methods may lose their effectiveness, others won't. Take personal one-to-one contact, for example. Sociologists tell us that while our society has become "high tech," people are wanting it to become "high touch." From medical treatment to personalized service at a store, many are tired of being treated like a number, a blip on the computer screen. There is something to be said for personal involvement.

The megachurches have learned this. You can talk to the staff at any of them. They will tell you that part of the secret for their growth are the scores of small groups—support groups, home Bible studies, and classes. There are countless small "congregations" within the larger congregation.

2. Don't fear what is new.

Those of us who are older are sometimes reluctant to change. We don't know about all this "new stuff." Some of us can't distinguish a floppy disk from a funky chicken. It's hard to keep up with all that's going on, but that doesn't mean we shouldn't try.

Consider some possibilities.

Try using a satellite dish to download a Christian video from Good News Productions, International, in Joplin, Missouri.

Try teleconferencing for a board meeting, instead of flying everyone across the country.

Use the church's web site as a tool to invite, to teach, to inform.

Send your church paper and prayer list via e-mail.

In all these ways and many more, we can utilize new methods while retaining the old message.

3. Don't forget the ultimate goal.

The world is lost without Jesus. We who have found Him need to share Him with others.

Our goal is not to build big churches, per se. Neither is it to try to keep up with—or outdo—our religious neighbors. We are to please Christ. We must bring people to obedient faith in Him. We must build congregations around the world that accurately represent His Word and His will.

The church has been called the only institution on earth that is concerned for those who are not members of it. We must not seek to please ourselves, but the One whom we serve. As we find better ways to evangelize, we must use them, but the way in which we do it is crucial.

We must understand our culture so well that we know how to approach people today. By living a life consistent with our profession, we earn the right to be heard. Then we must try to present the changeless message of New Testament Christianity in the very best way possible.

Like Paul, we must become "all things to all people that by all means we may save some" (1 Corinthians 9:19-23).

Like Peter, we must "live such good lives among the pagans that . . . they may see your good deeds and glorify God" (1 Peter 2:12).

Like Priscilla and Aquila, we must find those who have limitations in their understanding of Scripture and teach them the way of the Lord more perfectly (Acts 18:26).

Like Jesus taught His disciples, we must be "as shrewd as snakes and as innocent as doves" (Matthew 10:16).

Why should those who know God's truth be less effective in their presentation of it than those who tell Satan's lies? (Luke 16:8).

Are you willing to surrender the television, the magazine, the VCR, the newspaper, the radio, the telephone, and the computer to the enemy? Why can't God's people use every available tool to communicate the life-changing message of the gospel?

Let us resolve not to compromise what is essential, nor be dogmatic about what isn't.

ENDNOTES

1. *The Southeast Outlook* (Southeast Christian Church, Louisville, KY), August 7, 2003, 1.
2. Further information on the survey is available from the research center's Web site: **www.barna.org**.
3. See the chart, "Communication Methods between 1800–1900," in the appendix.
4. See the chart, "Additional Communication Methods from 1900–2000," in the appendix.

9

SPEAK THE TRUTH IN LOVE

A popular Jewish tale has a real lesson for us. Most Christians are familiar with the Shema. This prayer (recorded in Deuteronomy 6:4-9) begins, "Hear, O Israel; the Lord our God the Lord is one." According to the story, a sharp dispute arose in one ancient synagogue in Eastern Europe about how they should behave during the recitation of the Shema. Half of the worshipers insisted on standing, and the other half adamantly remained seated.

Those who were seated yelled at the others to sit down. The ones on their feet screamed at those in the pew, telling them to stand out of respect. You can imagine how these confrontations made it impossible for anyone to worship. The rabbi was at his wit's end. In desperation he went to visit a 98-year-old member of the synagogue, the only surviving founder of their temple.

"Is it the tradition to stand during prayer?" he began.

"No, that is not the tradition," the old gentleman replied quietly.

"So the tradition is really to sit?" the rabbi added.

"No, that is not the tradition."

Frustrated by this impasse, the rabbi wept. "My congregants fight all the time. Every time we gather to worship, they begin yelling at each other to sit or to stand—"

"Ah, yes," the old man interrupted him. "*That* is the tradition!"

Unfortunately, the story sounds all too familiar. Two mistaken views are prominent in the church today. Both are extreme.

LOVE WITHOUT TRUTH

Some believers are anxious that everyone be made to feel comfortable. No seeker should be confronted with such an unpleasant word as "sin." We must simply love everybody.

This approach is common in our world. It is politically incorrect to tell people they are wrong or mistaken. Some folks say, "As long as they are sincere, we should not confront them about their views."

Good-hearted, well-meaning people may love the Lord, but that does not mean they always teach according to the revealed truth of Scripture. You need only turn on the TV set, listen to the radio, or read current religious magazines to find many examples of this. These people love God; they are sincere, but they also may be mistaken on some points.

Jesus taught, "You will know the truth, and the truth will set you free" (John 8:32). Although the truth can hurt, not having the truth can hurt even more. If you are talking with your doctor, wouldn't you rather have him tell you honestly what your condition is? Who wants a physician that will sugarcoat the facts and fail to tell you the true status of your health? How can we think it is loving not to tell a person all that the Bible says he or she needs to do to go to Heaven?

The Bible says, "This is love: that we walk in obedience to his commands" (2 John 6). Jesus said, "If you love me, you will obey what I command" (John 14:6). If someone really loves Jesus, they will want to teach and practice whatever He said to do.

People who have love without truth need the truth. If we know the truth, we are responsible to share it with them. But when we do, we must represent not only the truth of Christ, but the love of Christ as well. Some others in our world are zealous for truth, but appear to lack love.

We must represent not only the truth of Christ, but the love of Christ as well.

TRUTH WITHOUT LOVE

We might think first of the Pharisees when this trait is mentioned, but this approach was not limited to them. The twelve disciples themselves didn't always display love, even though they were staunch advocates of the truth. One day John came to Jesus and reported, "Master, we saw a man driving out demons in your name and we tried to stop him, because he is not one of us" (Luke 9:49). The Savior replied, "Do not stop him, for whoever is not against you is for you" (v. 59).

Soon after this the disciples came to a Samaritan village that would not welcome them in. When James and John saw this, they asked, "Lord,

Speaking the Truth in Love

do you want us to call fire down from heaven to destroy them?" (Luke 9:54). Jesus quickly rebuked them. Why? Because in both instances, although the disciples had the truth, they didn't have love. Many of us behave in similar ways at times.

A preacher asked a Bible-school class of junior boys, "Now, fellows, when you go out to battle for the Lord, what weapon do you use in fighting sin?"

"I know that one," one boy piped up. "You hit 'em with the axe of the apostles!"

Sometimes we may use the book of Acts about that way! The book itself is truth, but making use of it as a weapon is not loving. And after all, isn't our purpose to get people to obey the truth? (1 Peter 1:22). Jesus wants us to win people, not arguments. If we come across to an unbelieving world as narrow sectarians who are proud to be "the New Testament church," we are in trouble. We have missed what Jesus wanted. People will not care how much we know until they know how much we care.

TRUTH IN LOVE

The solution, of course, is to blend the two qualities together. Paul said, "Speaking the truth in love, we will in all things grow up into him who is the Head, that is Christ" (Ephesians 4:15). The perfect example in this, as in everything else, is Jesus.

Jesus didn't compromise. He didn't water down the truth. He didn't soft-pedal it. He didn't change the message to fit the crowd or to try to attract a larger crowd. He stayed with the truth, but He spoke in love.

Remember His meeting with the rich, young ruler? Jesus gave that young man the hardest teaching he had ever heard. "Sell everything you have and give it to the poor." But how did Jesus say it? Mark tells us, "Jesus looked at him and loved him" (Mark 10:21). Truth in love.

Or see Him with the woman taken in adultery. He did not excuse her sin. He stood with the truth: adultery is wrong. But Jesus didn't stone her; He forgave her. "Neither do I condemn thee: go and sin no more" (John 8:11, King James Version). Truth in love.

And we could go on. Zacchaeus, Bartimaeus, the Samaritan woman, Peter—He handled all of them the same way. Speaking the truth in love includes not just what you say, but how you say it, and why you say it. Wayne B. Smith says, "I have never had to apologize for my position, but sometimes I have for my disposition."

The motto of Ozark Christian College says it well: "The Word of Christ taught in the Spirit of Christ." We need both. We must teach the truth of God's Word, but we don't have to be obnoxious, overbearing, and judgmental when we do it. The truth will offend some people, but let's be certain that it is the message, not the messenger, that turns a person off.

How should you tell a person the truth when you're afraid it's going to upset him? Try telling him just as you would tell someone you really care about—your spouse, your parent, your child. You don't want to hurt these people. You don't want to offend them. You want them to receive the message in the right way, because you care about their reaction. You love the person, but you have to tell them the truth.

Rubel Shelly describes the thoughtless way some Christians attack people in other churches, and quickly condemn folk who know nothing about Jesus. He wrote,

> Suppose you saw a three-year-old boy holding a razor-sharp knife by its blade. Would you yell? Grab the handle? Or gently offer something pretty and appealing in hope he would drop the dangerous knife for the sake of something safe and attractive?
>
> If there is someone with whom God has positioned you to share a kernel of truth, be careful going about it. Unless you are very Christlike in your approach, you may not only drive the person away from yourself, but destroy the possibility of his hearing the gospel.
>
> "And the Lord's servant must not quarrel; instead, he must be kind to everyone, able to teach, not resentful,' said Paul. 'Those who oppose him he must gently instruct, in the hope that God will grant them repentance leading them to a knowledge of the truth" (2 Timothy 2:24,25).[1]

To me one of the most beautiful illustrations of this is found in Acts 18. Here we meet Apollos, a sincere religious person. He was right about many things, but he was wrong on one point—baptism. Notice how Priscilla and Aquila treated him. When they heard Apollos speaking in the synagogue, they didn't cut him down or embarrass him in public. They talked to him privately, lovingly, kindly. What an example! They spoke the truth in love.

This is just the way Paul told the Galatians to do it. "Brothers, if someone is caught in a sin, you who are spiritual should restore him gently. But watch yourself, or you also may be tempted" (6:1).

Seth Wilson has said, "Sometimes we're more interested in sorting the brethren when we should be interested in serving them." God did not appoint us to be judges, but He did make us evangelists. We are stewards of His message. We must keep it pure. We must share it in love. As the old slogan puts it, "In matters of faith, unity; in matters of opinion, liberty; in all things, love."

Perhaps someday we could add another verse to the old hymn, "Blest Be the Tie":

> As we proclaim Your Word,
>   Grant wisdom from above,
> That always when we talk to men,
>   We'll speak the truth in love.

ENDNOTES

1. Rubel Shelly, *Love Lines* (Nashville: Woodmont Hills Church of Christ, February 12, 2003) 2.

C O N C L U S I O N

It's not easy trying to be "simply Christian."

But making the effort is worthwhile.

Many people in today's world are looking just for "basic Christianity." That's all they need and want—and that is exactly what we can offer. We must stay the course.

When Mark McGwire hit his record-breaking home run back in September 1998, my son Dave was watching the game on television. He described what happened. "Mark McGwire's son, the batboy, came up. With a smile from ear to ear, Mark picked up his son and lifted him into the sky. After an emotional hug, he pointed up in the stands to his father, because he didn't want him to be left out of the celebration."

Dave concluded, "I think the reason I was so moved by it was the simple fact that in the midst of his excitement, Mark acknowledged the past and the future, his father and his son. Basically that's the goal of every church leader. To look back and thank God for the good that has taken place, but not to live in the past. Instead we must live with integrity in the present, so that the Lord can continue to grow His church spiritually, relationally, and numerically."

Like Mark McGwire, we must remember the past, but keep looking to the future. If we lift up Jesus, He will draw all people to himself. Our challenge is to hold up the Son, and keep looking to the Father.

Let the church be the church our Lord wants it to be. Not different in any essential element. True to Scripture. Serving Him daily. Living in the hope of Heaven. Showing love to everyone. One day Jesus will return to claim His bride, the church. We must be ready! As the old hymn says,

> Till, with the vision glorious,
> her longing eyes are blest,
> And the great church victorious
> shall be the church at rest.

A P P E N D I X

Part One
Resources for Visitors/Seekers/New Members

Part Two
"What We Stand For" by James A. Garfield
"Who Are We?" by Lynn Gardner

Part Three
2003-04 Christian College Report (Christian Standard)

Part Four
2003 Megachurch Report (Christian Standard)

Part Five
"The Declaration and Address" by Thomas Campbell

Part Six
"How We Look to Others" (Editorial)
"An Outsider's View of the Restoration Movement"
by Jim Garlow

Part Seven
"Last Will and Testament of the Springfield
Presbytery"

Part Eight
Communication Methods in the Restoration Movement

PART ONE

Resources for Visitors/Seekers/New Members:

The Family of God. LeRoy Lawson. (60 pages, soft cover, $4.99). Available from College Press Publishing Company, 223 West 3rd Street, Joplin, MO 64801 (800/289-3300) **www.collegepress.com**.

Simply Christians. A 16-page reprint from *The Lookout.* Available from Standard Publishing, 8121 Hamilton Ave., Cincinnati, OH 45232. (800/482-2060). **www.standardpub.com**

What Kind of Church Is This? An 8-page reprint from *Christian Standard.* Available from Standard Publishing (address, phone #, and web address above).

Jesus, His Church, and You. An 8-page reprint from *Christian Standard.* Available from Standard Publishing (address, phone #, and web address above).

PART TWO

What We Stand For

James A. Garfield, former President of the United States, is one of the best-known individuals associated with Christian Churches and Churches of Christ. He even served as a "lay preacher." To answer the many questions he received about the group of believers with whom he worshiped, he wrote a classic statement. This copy is excerpted from Christian Standard, *November 14, 1993, and is used with permission.*

1. We call ourselves Christians, or Disciples of Christ. . . .

2. We believe in God the Father.

3. We believe that Jesus is the Christ, the Son of the living God, and our Savior. We regard the divinity of Christ as the fundamental truth of the Christian system.

4. We believe in the Holy Spirit, both as to His agency in conversion and as indwelling the heart of the Christian.

5. We accept both the Old and New Testament Scriptures as the inspired Word of God.

6. We believe in the future punishment of the wicked and the future reward of the righteous.

7. We believe that the Deity is a prayer hearing and a prayer answering God.

8. We observe the institution of the Lord's Supper on the Lord's Day. To this table we neither invite nor debar; we say it is the Lord's Supper for all of the Lord's children.

9. We plead for the union of God's people on the Bible and the Bible alone.

10. The Christ is our only creed.

11. We maintain that all the ordinances should be observed as they were in the days of the apostles.

WHO ARE WE?

At a Restoration Forum sponsored by Peace On Earth Ministries in 1994, Dr. Lynn Gardner, longtime dean of Ozark Christian College, gave a brief summary of basic convictions held by those in Christian Churches and Churches of Christ. His statement, reprinted below, represents a contemporary effort to introduce this fellowship of churches to others.

What are the beliefs of those in the Christian Churches and Churches of Christ?

We have no official doctrinal statement. I cannot speak for everyone. I will state what I believe are the doctrinal convictions of the majority in the Christian Churches and Churches of Christ. This is not meant to be a comprehensive statement, but rather a statement of basic convictions.

God is the eternal, sovereign creator and ruler of the universe. He is our holy, loving heavenly Father. He has revealed himself in Scripture.

Jesus is God in flesh. He was born of the virgin Mary. He worked miracles and fulfilled the Old Testament prophecies concerning the Messiah. He died for our sins and was raised from the dead. He will return to earth to be the judge of all men.

The Bible is completely true and is the inspired word of God written. . . . The New Testament is the authoritative standard for faith and practice. We have correctly understood the meaning of Scripture when we understand the biblical author's intended meaning.

We, as human beings, were created in the image of God and stand, either as sinners in need of salvation, or sinners saved by God's loving grace. We inherit the consequences of Adam's sin, but not the guilt. We are sinners because we choose to sin. We have free will to either accept or reject God's offered salvation. The New Testament plan of salvation includes faith in the deity and lordship of Jesus, repentance from one's sins, and immersion for forgiveness of sins. The Holy Spirit dwells within believers, helping us turn from the works of the flesh and produce the fruit of the Spirit in our lives.

The church as the body of Christ is God's chosen agency to seek the evangelization of the lost and the edification of Christians worldwide. Loving God's truth includes loving people. Each local congregation is autonomous, choosing its own elders, deacons and minister(s), answering to no authority other than the Word of God. Every Lord's Day Christians regularly assemble with other believers for preaching, breaking of bread, prayers and fellowship. Practicing the Christianity taught by Christ and the apostles in the New Testament is the basis for unity and evangelism.

PART THREE

2003-04 CHRISTIAN COLLEGE REPORT

For many years *Christian Standard* magazine has published an annual Christian College Report issue. Editor Mark Taylor has given permission to reproduce the chart from the magazine's March 21, 2004, edition in our appendix. This highlights the latest news from 36 schools for 2003-04.

	TYPE	FACULTY Full-time	Part-time	STUDENTS Male	Female	Full-time Equivalent*	2003 GRADS** Four-year	Other	TOTAL INCOME	TOTAL EXPENDITURES	ACCREDITATION
ALBERTA BIBLE COLLEGE Calgary, Alberta, Canada (403) 282-2994 X (403) 282-3084	BC	12	19	84	77	133	8	21	$1.02 million	$956,221	AABC (applicant)
ATLANTA CHRISTIAN COLLEGE East Point, Georgia (404) 761-8861 X (404) 669-2024	BC	20	33	182	208	350	62	5	$6.50 million	$6.66 million	SACS
BLUEFIELD COLLEGE OF EVANGELISM Bluefield, West Virginia (866) 825-5223 X (304) 589-6357	BC	4	9	16	2	10	10	0	$598,687	$589,957	
BOISE BIBLE COLLEGE Boise, Idaho (208) 376-7731 X (208) 376-7743	BC	7	8	53	60	119	14	17	$1.90 million	$1.88 million	AABC
CENTRAL CHRISTIAN COLLEGE OF THE BIBLE Moberly, Missouri (660) 263-3900 X (660) 263-3936	BC	9	14	142	99	230	23	12	$2.16 million	$2.03 million	AABC
CINCINNATI BIBLE COLLEGE Cincinnati, Ohio (513) 244-8100 X (513) 244-8140	BC	20	20	350	276	563	102	12	$9.92 million	$10.20 million	NCACS AABC
CINCINNATI BIBLE SEMINARY Cincinnati, Ohio (513) 244-8100 X (513) 244-8434	GS	10	9	187	109	225	0	65	Included with CBC	Included with CBC	NCACS ATS
COLEGIO BIBLICO Eagle Pass, Texas (830) 773-3110 X (830) 758-0710	BC	6	9	32	13	4	5	2	$735,781	$765,963	SAABC
COLLEGE OF THE SCRIPTURES Louisville, Kentucky (502) 451-4141	BC	2	2	4	4	1	0	0			
CROSSROADS COLLEGE Rochester, Minnesota (507) 288-4563 X (507) 288-9046	BC	11	13	57	56	103	14	19	$1.52 million	$1.93 million	AABC
DALLAS CHRISTIAN COLLEGE Dallas, Texas (972) 241-3371 X (972) 241-8021	BC	10	45	153	145	258	40	2	$3.27 million	$3.41 million	AABC

*FTE represents number of full-time students plus total part-time student hours divided by 12. **GRADS: These are estimates. TYPE: BC, Bible College; ES, External Studies; GS, Graduate Seminary; LA, Liberal Arts. ACCREDITATION: AABC, Accrediting Association of Bible Colleges; ATS, The Association for Theological Schools in the United States and Canada; CSWE, Council on Social Work Education; KCPE, Kentucky Council on Postsecondary Education; NASCU, (Oregon) Northwest Association of Schools, Colleges and Universities; NCACS, North Central Association of Colleges and Schools; SAABC, Southern Accrediting Association of Bible Colleges; SACS, Southern Association of Colleges and Schools; WASC, Western Association of Schools and Colleges.

	TYPE	FACULTY Full-time	Part-time	STUDENTS Male	Female	Full-time Equivalent*	2003 GRADS** Four-year	Other	TOTAL INCOME	TOTAL EXPENDITURES	ACCREDITATION
EMMANUEL SCHOOL OF RELIGION Johnson City, Tennessee (423) 926-1186 X (423) 926-6198	GS	7	5	122	37	129	0	28	$2.74 million	$3.39 million	ATS SACS
FLORIDA CHRISTIAN COLLEGE Kissimmee, Florida (407) 847-8966 X (407) 847-3925	BC	11	18	120	110	209	19	7	$3.59 million	$3.90 million	AABC SACS
GREAT LAKES CHRISTIAN COLLEGE Lansing, Michigan (517) 321-0242 X (517) 321-5902	BC	13	10	107	95	166	23	2	$3.28 million	$3.25 million	NCACS AABC
HOPE INTERNATIONAL UNIVERSITY Fullerton, California (714) 879-3901 X (714) 526-0360	LA,GS, ES	36	85	434	701	1,017	175	120	$19.35 million	$18.13 million	WASC
JOHNSON BIBLE COLLEGE Knoxville, Tennessee (865) 573-4517 X (865) 251-2336	BC	23	34	411	413	748	89	34	$9.31 million	$9.62 million	AABC SACS
KENTUCKY CHRISTIAN COLLEGE Grayson, Kentucky (606) 474-3000 X (606) 474-3132	BC,LA, GS	35	27	286	310	568	85	3	$10.62 million	$11.06 million	SACS CSWE
LINCOLN CHRISTIAN COLLEGE Lincoln, Illinois (217) 732-3168 X (217) 732-5718	BC	36	27	338	367	626	99	21	$9.56 million	$9.05 million	NCACS AABC
LINCOLN CHRISTIAN SEMINARY Lincoln, Illinois (217) 732-3168 X (217) 732-1821	GS	11	13	190	63	156	0	38	Included with LCC	Included with LCC	NCACS ATS
LINCOLN CHRISTIAN COLLEGE/ EAST COAST Bel Air, Maryland (410) 836-2000 X (410) 734-4271	BC	5	2	42	27	47	3	4	$535,000	$550,000	NCACS AABC
LOUISVILLE BIBLE COLLEGE Louisville, Kentucky (502) 231-5221 X (502) 231-5222	BC	0	22	199	103	69	4	12	$498,250	$473,848	KCPE
MANHATTAN CHRISTIAN COLLEGE Manhattan, Kansas (785) 539-3571 X (785) 539-0832	BC	8	22	172	190	284	75	5	$4.02 million	$4.07 million	NCACS AABC
MARITIME CHRISTIAN COLLEGE Charlottetown, PEI, Canada (902) 628-8887 X (902) 892-3959	BC	2	5	11	6	15	2	5	$325,248	$340,271	None
MID-SOUTH CHRISTIAN COLLEGE Memphis, Tennessee (901) 375-4400 X (901) 375-4085	BC	3	14	27	11	12	3	0	$320,000	$310,000	None
MILLIGAN COLLEGE Milligan College, Tennessee (423) 461-8719 X (423) 461-8954	LA	66	35	286	425	824	174	78	$14.05 million	$13.41 million	SACS
NEBRASKA CHRISTIAN COLLEGE Norfolk, Nebraska (402) 379-5000 X (402) 379-5100	BC	5	11	88	82	161	14	16	$1.92 million	$2.05 million	AABC

	TYPE	FACULTY Full-time	Part-time	STUDENTS Male	Female	Full-time Equivalent*	2003 GRADS** Four-year	Other	TOTAL INCOME	TOTAL EXPENDITURES	ACCREDITATION
NORTHWEST CHRISTIAN COLLEGE Eugene, Oregon (541) 343-1641 X (541) 343-9159	LA	25	50	204	311	457	130	30	NA	NA	NASCU
OZARK CHRISTIAN COLLEGE Joplin, Missouri (417) 624-2518 X (417) 624-0090	BC	29	36	414	385	730	86	46	$7.68 million	$7.47 million	AABC
PLATTE VALLEY BIBLE COLLEGE Scottsbluff, Nebraska (308) 632-6933 X (308) 632-8599	BC	5	4	26	22	36	3	16	NA	NA	None
PUGET SOUND CHRISTIAN COLLEGE Mountlake Terrace, Washington (425) 775-8686 X (425) 775-8688	BC	8	16	71	88	147	25	10	$5.50 million	$3.30 million	AABC
ROANOKE BIBLE COLLEGE Elizabeth City, North Carolina (252) 334-2070 X (252) 334-2071	BC	10	5	112	82	169	26	6	$2.69 million	$2.40 million	AABC SACS
SAINT LOUIS CHRISTIAN COLLEGE Florissant, Missouri (314) 837-6777 X (314) 837-8291	BC	10	23	135	99	194	28	5	$2.73 million	$2.72 million	AABC
SAN JOSE CHRISTIAN COLLEGE San Jose, California (408) 278-4300 X (408) 293-7352	BC	15	37	197	164	327	55	7	$5.32 million	$5.51 million	AABC WASC
SUMMIT THEOLOGICAL SEMINARY Peru, Indiana (765) 472-4111 X (765) 472-4111	BC, GS,ES	1	13	724	220	NA	6	10	$220,511	$216,666	None
WINSTON-SALEM BIBLE COLLEGE Winston-Salem, North Carolina (336) 744-0900 X (336) 744-0901	BC	2	7	29	13	28	5	3	$492,105	$483,518	AABC (candidate)

PART FOUR

2003 MEGACHURCH REPORT

Christian Standard magazine annually publishes a list of all of the Christian Churches and Churches of Christ that averaged 1000 or more in attendance during the previous year. The March 7, 2004, edition listed 97 churches. After the publication date, the magazine received reports from 5 more congregations. (These were then reported in the April 25 issue.) Managing Editor Jim Nieman has incorporated the additional names into a single composite list for our appendix. We are reprinting this copyrighted material with permission. The list includes a grand total of 102 megachurches for the year 2003.

Church	Attendance	Baptisms	Transfers	City	Minister
SOUTHEAST CHRISTIAN	17,971	1,191	996	Louisville, KY	Bob Russell
CHRIST'S CHURCH OF THE VALLEY	8,227	583	631	Peoria, AZ	Donald J. Wilson
SOUTHLAND CHRISTIAN	8,000	NA	NA	Lexington, KY	Jon Weece
CENTRAL CHRISTIAN	7,020	671	306	Henderson, NV	Jud Wilhite
SHEPHERD OF THE HILLS	5,200	382	385	Porter Ranch, CA	Dudley C. Rutherford
CENTRAL CHRISTIAN	5,159	372	NA	Mesa, AZ	Cal Jernigan
CROSSROADS CHRISTIAN	5,023	437	129	Corona, CA	Barry McMurtrie
ADVENTURE CHRISTIAN	4,498	185	NA	Roseville, CA	Rick Stedman
CANYON RIDGE CHRISTIAN	3,876	342	100	Las Vegas, NV	Kevin Odor
OVERLAKE CHRISTIAN	3,617	128	NA	Redmond, WA	Richard Kingham
EAST 91ST STREET CHRISTIAN	3,246	156	87	Indianapolis, IN	Derek Duncan
MANDARIN CHRISTIAN	3,206	263	NA	Jacksonville, FL	Dennis A. Bratton
COMMUNITY CHRISTIAN	3,200	239	NA	Naperville, IL	Dave Ferguson
CENTRAL CHRISTIAN	3,194	210	309	Wichita, KS	Joe Wright
CHRIST'S CHURCH OF THE VALLEY	3,166	208	NA	San Dimas, CA	Chuck Booher
CROSSROADS CHRISTIAN	3,109	249	183	Evansville, IN	Bill Peroni
NORTHSIDE CHRISTIAN	3,097	207	212	New Albany, IN	George Ross
REAL LIFE MINISTRIES	3,015	500+	NA	Post Falls, ID	Jim Putnam
LIFEBRIDGE CHRISTIAN	3,000	194	124	Longmont, CO	Rick Rusaw
PARAMOUNT TERRACE CHRISTIAN	2,828	145	173	Amarillo, TX	C. Scott Greer
SAVANNAH CHRISTIAN	2,824	269	372	Savannah, GA	Cam Huxford
HARVESTER CHRISTIAN	2,708	154	175	St. Charles, MO	Ben Merold
SOUTHBROOK CHRISTIAN	2,700	103	NA	Centerville, OH	Charlie McMahan
EASTVIEW CHRISTIAN	2,605	158	75	Normal, IL	Gary York
SHERWOOD OAKS CHRISTIAN	2,503	99	64	Bloomington, IN	Tom Ellsworth
CHANDLER CHRISTIAN	2,425	256	190	Chandler, AZ	Roger Storms
EASTSIDE CHRISTIAN	2,300	160	185	Fullerton, CA	Graydon Jessup
MOUNT PLEASANT CHRISTIAN	2,300	177	106	Greenwood, IN	Chris Philbeck
BROWNSBURG CHRISTIAN	2,290	147	151	Brownsburg, IN	Steven T. Reeves
NORTHEAST CHRISTIAN	2,290	207	84	Louisville, KY	Bob Cherry
KNOTT AVENUE CHRISTIAN	2,280	194	NA	Anaheim, CA	Shane Womack
OWENSBORO CHRISTIAN	2,239	139	131	Owensboro, KY	Myke Templeton
INDIAN CREEK CHRISTIAN	2,231	152	150	Indianapolis, IN	Gary L. Johnson
FIRST CHURCH OF CHRIST	2,229	79	122	Burlington, KY	L.D. Campbell
PANTANO CHRISTIAN	2,217	103	NA	Tucson, AZ	Timothy A. Coop
SOUTHEAST CHRISTIAN	2,100	118	200	Parker, CO	Todd Hudson
NORTHSIDE CHRISTIAN	2,078	222	280	Clovis, CA	David N. Rutherford

Church	Attendance	Baptisms	Transfers	City	Minister
BEAVERTON CHRISTIAN	2,058	127	88	Beaverton, OR	Clark H. Tanner
KINGSWAY CHRISTIAN	2,049	145	211	Indianapolis, IN	John Caldwell
FIRST CHRISTIAN	2,031	121	75	Huntington Beach, CA	Bruce Templeton
FAIRFIELD CHRISTIAN	2,010	150	111	Lancaster, OH	Russell Johnson
ROCKY MOUNTAIN CHRISTIAN	2,010	139	110	Niwot, CO	Alan Ahlgrim
CENTRAL CHRISTIAN	2,000	206	NA	Lancaster, CA	David Prather
PARKCREST CHRISTIAN	2,000	155	57	Long Beach, CA	Roger Beard
MOUNTAIN CHRISTIAN	1,992	247	111	Joppa, MD	Ben Cachiaras
CROSSROADS CHRISTIAN	1,911	171	168	Arlington, TX	Barry L. Cameron
FIRST CHRISTIAN	1,911	119	98	Canton, OH	John A. Hampton
WESTLINK CHRISTIAN	1,894	135	NA	Wichita, KS	N. Gene Carlson
CHRIST'S CHURCH OF ORONOGO	1,850	85	61	Oronogo, MO	Lynn R. Ragsdale
WEST SIDE CHRISTIAN	1,793	132	145	Springfield, IL	Eddie Lowen
TRADERS POINT CHRISTIAN	1,784	86	88	Indianapolis, IN	Howard R. Brammer
RIVERTREE CHRISTIAN	1,752	150	140	Massillon, OH	Greg Nettle
NORTHSHORE CHRISTIAN	1,684	112	NA	Everett, WA	
RAINIER VIEW CHRISTIAN	1,661	126	93	Tacoma, WA	Roger Worsham
NORTHERN HILLS CHRISTIAN	1,660	200+	NA	Brighton, CO	Dennis Thomas
GREENWOOD CHRISTIAN	1,565	86	86	Greenwood, IN	Shan Rutherford
FAITH CHRISTIAN COMMUNITY	1,550	60	NA	Anchorage, AK	Steve Holsinger
COLLEGE HEIGHTS CHRISTIAN	1,543	58	99	Joplin, MO	Randy Gariss
CENTRAL CHRISTIAN	1,527	85	39	Beloit, WI	David L. Clark
PARKVIEW CHRISTIAN	1,519	111	117	Orland Park, IL	Tim Harlow
CROSSROADS CHRISTIAN	1,482	34	78	Lexington, KY	Glen Schneiders
PLAINFIELD CHRISTIAN	1,476	79	78	Plainfield, IN	Stephen K. White
FIRST CHRISTIAN	1,474	166	114	Kernersville, NC	Peter L. Kunkle
HIGHLAND MEADOWS CHRISTIAN	1,466	151	165	Colleyville, TX	Drew Sherman
CHRIST'S CHURCH AT MASON	1,438	97	106	Mason, OH	Tom Moll
MARYLAND COMMUNITY	1,390	50	NA	Terre Haute, IN	Vince McFarland
SUNNYBROOK CHRISTIAN	1,388	36	88	Stillwater, OK	Jim Johnson
SPRING OF LIFE CHRISTIAN	1,382	100	NA	Mesa, AZ	Kevin Carlson
LAKESIDE CHRISTIAN	1,309	66	78	Lakeside Park, KY	John Russell
CHAPEL ROCK CHRISTIAN	1,300	50	60	Indianapolis, IN	Fred Rodkey
JOURNEY CHRISTIAN	1,289	134	172	Apopka, FL	Dan Donaldson
COUNTRYSIDE CHRISTIAN	1,250	104	83	Michigan City, IN	Richard Jones
FIRST COLONY	1,250	48	92	Sugar Land, TX	Ronnie Norman
GREENFORD CHRISTIAN	1,240	86	60	Greenford, OH	Jeff Hugus
WHITE OAK CHRISTIAN	1,211	104	59	Cincinnati, OH	David Roberson
FIRST CHRISTIAN	1,209	87	108	Fort Myers, FL	Gary Cox
PIKES PEAK CHRISTIAN	1,205	119	NA	Colorado Springs, CO	Bryan Myers
PINEDALE CHRISTIAN	1,203	109	62	Winston-Salem, NC	Bill McKenzie
OKOLONA CHRISTIAN	1,202	90	111	Louisville, KY	Dave Hastings
FIRST CHRISTIAN	1,200	95	94	Johnson City, TN	Tim Wallingford
SUMMIT CHRISTIAN	1,200	97	NA	Sparks, NV	Steve Bond
YUCAIPA CHRISTIAN	1,197	66	19	Yucaipa, CA	Don S. Hinkle
CHERRY LANE CHRISTIAN	1,174	83	92	Meridian, ID	Steve Moore
FIRST CHRISTIAN	1,153	75	87	Florissant, MO	Charles D. Wingfield
CHRIST'S CH. OF FLAGSTAFF	1,128	121	91	Flagstaff, AZ	James Dorman
FIRST CHRISTIAN	1,100	92	100	Tarpon Springs, FL	Greg Johnson
THE CHURCH AT MT. GILEAD	1,096	101	107	Mooresville, IN	Jeff Faull
FIRST CHRISTIAN	1,068	112	83	Newburgh, IN	Mike Claypool
EASTSIDE CHRISTIAN	1,062	NA	NA	Milford, OH	Will Mullins
FIRST CHRISTIAN	1,062	46	62	Scottsburg, IN	Phil LaMaster
CAPITOL CITY CHRISTIAN	1,059	60	50	Lincoln, NE	Bill Thornton
WORTHINGTON CHRISTIAN	1,054	49	72	Columbus, OH	Marshall Hayden

Church	Attendance	Baptisms	Transfers	City	Minister
ROLLING HILLS CHRISTIAN	1,047	103	NA	El Dorado Hills, CA	Jeff Bigelow
FIRST CHRISTIAN	1,043	97	87	Yuma, AZ	Daniel E. Trautman
NEW LIFE CHRISTIAN	1,035	86	NA	Centreville, VA	Brett Andrews
BRIGHT CHRISTIAN	1,023	134	83	Bright, IN	Mark Fugate
HARBORSIDE CHRISTIAN	1,015	59	65	Clearwater, FL	Dan Stuecher
FIRST CHRISTIAN	1,012	54	17	Springfield, OH	Dale Holzbauer
COMMUNITY CHRISTIAN	1,010	103	87	Fort Lauderdale, FL	Scott Eynon
VALLEY VIEW CHRISTIAN	1,006	30	49	Dallas, TX	Ron Key
SOUTHERN ACRES CHRISTIAN	1,002	70	46	Lexington, KY	Wally Rendel
MISSION VIEJO CHRISTIAN	1,000	31	20	Mission Viejo, CA	Mike Maiolo

PART FIVE

THE DECLARATION AND ADDRESS

The following is part of a document created by Thomas Campbell and completed on September 7, 1809. The entire document, the "Declaration and Address," was a 56-page pamphlet consisting of four parts. (1) The Declaration stating briefly the reasons for organization of the Christian Association of Washington and proposing a tentative constitution; (2) the Address, setting forth in logical form the principles of Christian unity and the means by which it might be attained. (3) the Appendix in which certain points in the Address are amplified and possible criticisms are answered; and (4) a Postscript suggesting steps that should be taken for the promotion of the crusade.

This material is in the public domain and is widely available on the Web.

Let none imagine that the subjoined propositions are at all intended as an overture towards a new creed, or standard, for the church, or, as in any wise designed to be made a term of communion;—nothing can be farther from our intention. They are merely designed for opening up the way, that we may come fairly and firmly to original grounds upon clear and certain premises: and take up things just as the Apostles left them—That thus disentangled from the accruing embarrassments of intervening ages, we may stand with evidence upon the same ground on which the church stood in the beginning—Having said so much to solicit attention and prevent mistake, we submit as follows.

Proposition 1. That the church of Christ upon earth is essentially, intentionally, and constitutionally one; consisting of all those in every place that profess their faith in Christ and obedience to Him in all things according to the Scriptures, and that manifest the same by their tempers and conduct, and of none else as none else can be truly and properly called Christians.

Proposition 2. That although the church of Christ upon earth must necessarily exist in particular and distinct societies, locally separate one from another; yet there ought to be no schisms, no uncharitable divisions among them. They ought to receive each other as Christ Jesus hath also received them to the glory of God. And for this purpose, they ought all to walk by the same rule, to mind and speak the same thing; and to be perfectly joined together in the same mind, and the same judgment.

Proposition 3. That in order to do this, nothing ought to be inculcated upon Christians as articles of faith; nor required of them as terms of communion; but what is expressly taught and enjoined upon them, in the Word of God.

Nor ought any thing be admitted, as of divine obligation, in their church constitution and managements, but what is expressly enjoined by the authority of our Lord Jesus Christ and His Apostles upon the New Testament church; either in express terms, or by approved precedent.

Proposition 4. That although the scriptures of the Old and New Testament are inseparably connected, making together but one perfect and entire revelation of the Divine will, for the edification and salvation of the church; and therefore belongs to their immediate object, the New Testament is as perfect a constitution for the worship, discipline and government of the New Testament church, and as perfect a rule for the particular duties of its members; as the Old Testament was for the worship, discipline and government of the Old Testament church, and the particular duties of its members.

Proposition 5. That with respect to the commands and ordinances of our Lord Jesus Christ, where the Scriptures are silent, as to the express time or manner of performance, if any such there be; no human authority has power to interfere, in order to supply the supposed deficiency, by making laws for the church; nor can anything more be required of Christians in such cases, but only what they so observe these commands and ordinances, as will evidently answer the declared and obvious end of their institution. Much less has any human authority power to impose new commands or ordinances upon the church which our Lord Jesus Christ has not enjoined. Nothing ought to be received into the faith or worship of the church; or be made a term of communion among Christians, that is not as old as the New Testament.

Proposition 6. That although inferences and deductions from scripture premises, when fairly inferred, may be truly called the doctrine of God's Holy Word: Yet are they not formally binding upon the consciences of Christians farther than they perceive the connection, and evidently see that they are so; for their faith must not stand in the wisdom of men; but in the power and veracity of God—therefore no such deduction can be made terms of communion, but do properly belong to the after and progressive edification of the church. Hence it is evident that no such deductions or inferential truths ought to have any place in the church's confession.

Proposition 7. That although doctrinal exhibitions of the great system of divine truths, and defensive testimonies in opposition to prevailing errors, be highly expedient; and the more full and explicit they be, for those purposes, the better; yet as these must be in a great measure the effect of human reasoning, and of course must contain many inferential truths, they ought not to be made terms of Christian communion: unless we suppose, what is contrary to fact, that none have a right to the communion of the church, but such as possess a very clear and decisive judgment; or are come to a very high degree of doctrinal information; whereas the church from the beginning did, and ever will, consist of little children and young men, as well as fathers.

Proposition 8. That as it is not necessary that persons should have a particular knowledge or distinct apprehension of all divinely revealed truths in order to entitle them to place in the church; neither should they, for this purpose, be required to make a profession more extensive than their knowledge: but that, on the contrary, their having a due measure of scriptural self-knowledge respecting their lost and perishing condition by nature and practice; and of the way of salvation through Jesus Christ, accompanied with a profession of their faith in, and obedience to Him, in all things according to His Word, is all that is necessary to qualify them for admission into His Church.

Proposition 9. That all that are enabled, through grace, to make such a profession, and to manifest the reality of it in their tempers and conduct, should consider each other as the precious saints of God, should love each other as brethren, children of the same family and father, temples of the same spirit, members of the same body, subjects of the same grace, objects of the same divine love, bought with the same price, and joint heirs of the same inheritance. Whom God hath thus joined together, no man should dare to put asunder.

Proposition 10. That division among Christians is a horrid evil, fraught with many evils. It is antichristian, as it destroys the visible unity of the body of Christ; as if He were divided against Himself, excluding and excommunicating a part of Himself. It is antiscriptural, as being strictly prohibited by His sovereign authority; a direct violation of His express command. It is antinatural, as it excites Christians to condemn, to hate and oppose one another, who are bound by the highest and most endearing obligations to love each other as brethren, even as Christ has loved them. In a word, it is productive of confusion and of every evil work.

Proposition 11. That, in some instances, a partial neglect of the expressly revealed will of God; and, in others, an assumed authority for making the approbation of human opinions, and human inventions, a term of communion, by introducing them into the constitution, faith of worship, of the Church; are and have been, the immediate, obvious and universally acknowledged causes, of all the corruption's and divisions that ever have taken place in the Church of God.

Proposition 12. That all that is necessary to the highest state of perfection and purity of the church upon earth is, first, that none be received as members, but such as having that due measure of scriptural self-knowledge described above, do profess their faith in Christ and obedience to Him in all things according to Scriptures; nor, secondly, that any be retained in her communion longer than they continue to manifest the reality of their profession by their tempers and conduct. Thirdly, that her ministers, duly and Scripturally qualified, inculcate none other things than those very articles of faith and holiness expressly revealed and enjoined in the Word of God. Lastly, that in all their administrations they keep close by the observance of all divine ordinances, after the example of the primitive church, exhibited in the New Testament; without any additions whatsoever of human opinions or inventions of men.

Proposition 13. Lastly. That if any circumstantials indispensably necessary to the observance of divine ordinances be not found upon the page of express revelation, such, and such only, as are absolutely necessary for this purpose, should be adopted, under the title of human expedients, without any pretense to a more sacred origin;—so that any subsequent alteration or difference in the observance of these things might produce no contention nor division in the church.

PART SIX

AN OUTSIDER'S VIEW OF THE RESTORATION MOVEMENT

At the North American Christian Convention held in Columbus, Ohio, in 2002, Jim Garlow spoke for a workshop on the theme, "An Outsider's View of the Restoration Movement." Excerpts of his message were later printed in Christian Standard *(November 10, 2002). Following are first the editorial which I wrote to accompany it, and then the presentation by Garlow itself. Both are copyrighted by Standard Publishing, and are being reprinted here with permission.*

Editorial (*Christian Standard*)
How We Look to Others

The famous poet Robert Burns prayed that the gods would give us the gift "to see ourselves as others see us." It can be extremely valuable to learn what others think about you. We may feel that they have an inaccurate or incomplete view at times, and that may be true. But we need to understand how we appear to them. Then we must ask ourselves why they see us in this way. What do we do and say that gives them this impression? Such insights can be most helpful.

It was in that spirit that the leaders of this year's North American Christian Convention invited Jim Garlow to lead a workshop. They assigned him the topic, "An Outsider's View of the Restoration Movement." He ministers with Skyline Wesleyan Church near San Diego, California. Garlow grew up knowing little about our churches, but came upon Alexander Campbell in his graduate studies at Princeton Theological Seminary in New Jersey. That initial contact prompted him to want to learn more about this fellowship of churches.

In his presentation he affirmed the principles for which Campbell stood. He commended us in trying to practice New Testament Christianity today. In this issue we present excerpts from his workshop. Garlow included several specific suggestions he feels might be helpful. All of them are worth considering, even when we may disagree with them.

We are not ready, for example, to accept his suggestion that we refer to Campbell as our "founder," much as we appreciate Campbell's influence. But Garlow shows clearly that we need to explain the reasons for our reluctance to do that with tact and sensitivity, not abrasiveness and pride.

We are also reluctant to accept his suggestion that we call this fellowship of churches a denomination. Our intention remains simply to be what those first converts on the Day of Pentecost were—just Christians. As we do, however, we must guard against a sectarian spirit. We are not the totality of the Lord's church. All who obey the gospel are part of God's family whether they have ever heard of the Restoration Movement or not. We want to avoid separating ourselves from other believers, but reach out to them in love. We must continue to urge all Christians to be "Christians only."

Garlow's remarks affirm the validity of what we are trying to do as Christ's followers. The successes he notes indicate that we need not have a low self-image. We are doing many things right. God has blessed our efforts with growth, as we have sought to honor Him.

Brother Garlow has challenged us to be what we claim to be and to hold tightly to our ideals. For that we are most grateful.

—Sam E. Stone

An Outsider's View of the Restoration Movement
Jim Garlow

Why should a person care what someone outside the movement thinks? Because an outsider should bring some perspective that others who are in the movement do not have.

The independent Christian Churches need to be known more for what they are for . . .

My Background

On one occasion, John Wimber was asked to speak to the leadership of the Church of the Nazarene, as an "outsider." One of the Nazarene leaders said to him, "Tell us what you honestly think of us." Fifteen minutes later the person wished he had never asked that!

John hemmed and hawed for some time. Finally he said, "Well, I see you this way. You are like a basketball team. Uniformed, fine form, great athleticism, tremendous basketball skills, running up and down the court— but, in your gymnasium, you have no hoops on either end." I still don't know what he meant by that, but I assumed it wasn't a compliment.

Well, I think you have hoops, and I think you're hitting them. Quite candidly, I come as an affirmer of who you are.

I was a student at Princeton (New Jersey) Theological Seminary when I "discovered" Alexander Campbell. I am an amateur historian and I have been very intrigued for years about how to equip and mobilize laity for ministry. In the course of my study at Princeton, I came across Campbell. I didn't learn about him from someone in the Restoration Movement or a Christian church pastor somewhere. I said, "Wow! I like this guy!" I really enjoyed his feistiness, his directness. I feel that, over the course of time, I have come to know him and his personality just a little bit. I wish I had known many of you and could have asked you questions about him.

I put together a Lay Ministry Congress in 1980 and then again in 1982. We invited people from all over the country to talk about how to equip and mobilize people for ministry. I produced a videotape for it. On the tape I brought together actors portraying historical figures, much like Steve Allen did—a sort of a "meeting of the minds." These were figures from history I thought would have something significant to say to each other if they could all be in the room together.

We did some typecasting for these six figures—all movers and shakers of church history. The six figures included St. Francis of Assisi, Martin Luther, John Wesley, John R. Mott (Student Volunteer Movement), and Pope John 23rd. The other person was Alexander Campbell. He is the least known of the six, and I don't know why.

We had the most fun with him of anyone. The actors looked like these people. They were dressed for their era and, as I introduced them, they walked onto the stage. Campbell immediately—true to form—got into a very intriguing dialogue with the pope! I calmed him down before the two duked it out. At one point Campbell told Luther, "Luther, you didn't go far enough! If you'd just gone farther you could've cleaned up this mess. You stopped short!" St. Francis, so upset at the conflict, would lay down the rabbit he was holding in his lap and calm Campbell down every few minutes.

My Observations

I fell in love with Alexander Campbell. I wish I knew him as well as you do. Along with Luther and Wesley, I regard Campbell as one of my "friends."

But you did not ask me here to talk about Alexander Campbell. You have asked me to give an "outsider's" view. So here are some random observations regarding your movement:

1. Tell your story.

Tell it and tell it more often. No person is dead until you stop saying their name and telling their stories. If I'm around people very long, I work into the conversation the story of a man named Burtis Garlow. He's my dad. He died four years ago. I want everybody to know him. He's the greatest man on earth. I don't let him die because I tell his name and I use his stories. You need to tell the stories of Alexander Campbell—and tell them better, and tell them often. There is a richness in your heritage that I think is fascinating, especially in light of the postdenominational era in which we live. A whole lot of "postmoderns," the Gen-X generation, would be fascinated with the language of Campbell.

2. Tell it better.

I did an Internet search on Alexander Campbell. What I found over and over was what he was "against." This is where I think there has been failure in telling the story. Campbell was against some things, but he was for some things too. As a debater, he was admittedly more polemic than he was irenic. But the story should tell what he stood for, not just what he was against. The independent Christian Churches need to be known more for what they are for as they tell the story better.

There is a very engaging way to talk about Campbell from the standpoint of the authenticity he called for. That has a real ringing sound with the postmodern generation. If possible, always tell your story without condemning other theological groupings. Try to phrase it in this way: Campbell said, "There's a better way."

3. Don't be afraid of using the word "founder."

I was on a plane with a member of the Church of Christ. I said to him, "I really enjoy your founder, Alexander Campbell." That man almost threw me off the plane. I was never so underappreciated in my life! He said, "I want you to know we have no founder but Jesus." I didn't know what to say to that. I said, "Oh . . . OK," and that ended our conversation. I had wanted to engage in conversation about some things I find fascinating about Campbell. But, I didn't.

I grew up in the Wesleyan church. My dad always felt that a denomination should not be named after a man. That troubled him, even though we loved Wesley. We had no choice in the matter, so we went on with it. It wasn't a truly "big deal." Don't be afraid of using the word "founder" in a healthy way.

4. Don't be afraid of the word "denomination."

I suppose someone will disagree with me, and (tongue in cheek) you have the right to be wrong. Let me tell you why I'm saying that. I struggled for a long time asking, "Why did God ever allow denominations?" He must look down sometimes and think, "Oh, if My kids could just come to the same family reunion, it would be sweet." It would make you brokenhearted to be a parent and have your kids all go to 18 different family reunions. But . . . I'm so glad the body of Christ is bigger than just my theological grouping.

Like most people in my generation, I have a "postdenominational" mind-set. But back to the original question: Why does God even allow denominations? Answer: He allows people to "cluster" together who see some component of Himself. Now they don't have the whole picture, but they do have a piece of it, and they latch on to that piece really well. Their task in the economy of God's history, it appears to me, is to protect that part of the truth until the rest of the body of Christ is ready for it.

I grew up in a denomination where, because of our emphasis on a particular doctrine (sanctification) and our definition of "holiness," I rather assumed as a child that people from other groupings wouldn't make it to Heaven. The byword was, "Without holiness no man shall see the Lord." The only way I knew to get holiness was in my denomination.

It was quite a jolt when I realized, "Oh my—these other people love Jesus just like I do. They're saved too." That "wrecked" my whole theology. I began to see how much I could learn from various groupings. It enriched my experience and walk with the Lord and it enhanced my love for Him. Each denomination understood profoundly one component of God's nature . . . and I could learn from them all!

You, as Restorationists, bring to the table a real clarion call for unity. You really challenge us to bring down the barriers. You bring a clarion call to return to the purity and pristine beauty of the Word, and let the Word speak on how we "do" church. That's your contribution. Keep saying that. But understand that the walls of the denominations are falling, and those distinctives of various denominations are becoming less evident. Some of you refer to yourselves as a "nondenominational denomination."

That's a long adjective. Why not just drop it and admit you are, by a certain definition, a denomination.

5. You really are a movement.

A speaker at the Holiness Movement convention jolted his listeners a few years ago when he said, "The Holiness Movement is dead." It touched off a firestorm of debate. We had to look in the mirror and say, "In terms of the definition of what a movement is, we are no longer a movement." (A movement starts small and ends big. A program starts big and ends small. That's the difference.) As much as we hated to admit it, the Holiness Movement, as a movement, was dead.

You are a movement. You're ongoing. The Charismatic Movement of the 1970s and '80s cannot be called a movement today (in the United States), in the same way it was then. It was a movement. The Jesus Movement of the early 1970s was a movement. But you are a movement. You seem to have a second wind somehow, and I'm intrigued by this. I don't know your history well enough to know how you did it, but you have a renewed vigor and are spreading at an amazing pace.

I'm amazed to find churches of 14,000 like Southeast Christian Church in Louisville, Kentucky. Until the last few years, you have not been known outside of your arenas. You have churches of 8,000, 7,000, 6,500.

It's very energizing to see what is happening. You are a movement, and that's a great thing.

I do not know any other movement in the history of Christianity (certainly not in the American culture) that sprang out of an unusual form of recruitment—the debates. You were not driven by revival in your earliest days (like many denominations), but were formed out of debates. Where did the debates pull people from? Other churches. James O'Kelly was a Methodist. Eli Smith was a Baptist. Barton Stone was Presbyterian.

This was the same way the Charismatic Movement did in the 1970s and early '80s. But by the mid-'80s, the Charismatic Movement had pulled everybody they could from those churches. The niche in the marketplace had been absorbed. Now if they want to grow large churches, they have to figure out a way to convert the "pagans," instead of just extracting people from other churches.

Somehow you have turned that corner—from merely getting people from other churches (as you did in the mid-1800s) to really evangelizing the lost. Some of your megachurches are profoundly skilled in doing exactly what the original call of God is: to get the gospel out and present Jesus in such a compelling fashion so that people will respond. As you know, in your churches above 500 in attendance, the majority of people attending do not know anything about the background of the Christian Churches. They are new and fresh to your movement.

6. Megachurches have found a way to communicate.

If I took all of your churches that are over 1,000 and all the Baptist churches that are over 1,000, and the Nazarene churches over 1,000, you would find those megachurches have more in common with each other than they do with their respective movements. They all think alike, although they all choose to identify with their theological tradition.

What does that mean? If you're a Nazarene and you have a big church, you would like to say, "It's growing because of our emphasis upon sanctification." Baptists would say because of immersion. Charismatics would say because of the emphasis on gifts. But in reality, these megachurches are growing because they have powerful communicators who have found the key to presenting Christ in a compelling fashion

This really is an affirmation. What these churches all have in common is that they are very Jesus-centered. Part of the calling of Alexander Campbell was trans-denominationalism. I think he would be quite thrilled to see denominational barriers falling today.

7. Being a "New Testament church" is challenging.

This may be old news to you, but be aware that every theological clustering (euphemism for "denomination") really thinks that their church is "New Testament" as well. I'm not saying they are; I'm saying they think they are. I have never met a person in any denomination who says, "No, we are not a New Testament church." So when you claim to be as New Testament as you are, I think you do a much better job actually laying it out. Alexander

Campbell was brilliant. I don't know who in his time frame was exegetically brighter.

But when you talk about being a "New Testament church," bear in mind that every denomination feels it is. John Wesley believed the "people called Methodist" (as he called them) were a "primitive church." This is another way of saying "a New Testament church." I grew up in a vibrant church, and we thought we were New Testament. I look back now at our church government, and it really lacked a lot. We were American Democratic, but I don't know how New Testament our governmental structures actually were.

In my study of church governmental structure, it appears to me that in the New Testament church, one finds a series of models, as opposed to one singular "model." It depends what time frame you want to look at. In Jerusalem, they were communal—sharing everything they had. When is the last time you gave away everything you had to everybody else in the church? But at Antioch, they didn't do that. In Acts, it was "gift-based" leadership. In Paul's later writings, one finds much more structure. In Philippi, they were loving. In Corinth, they were lawless. A truly "New Testament church" is not easy to define. It depends what time frame you choose—early New Testament, or later New Testament—and which city you examine.

What does it mean to be a "New Testament church"? I would urge you to continue to use the expression, but use it with a sense of caution, because it's harder to get at that than most of us might imagine.

8. Maintain the role of all believers in ministry.

I don't know if you realize the intensity with which Alexander Campbell felt this. This is what attracted me to him. In his debate in 1843, in Lexington, Kentucky, with N.L. Rice, the Presbyterians bought the rights to it so they could print it. Rice was a powerful communicator and had everybody laughing. They thought that Mr. Rice had won the day. The Presbyterians widely disseminated the transcript of the debate. But when people would read it in the quietness of their home, they all were won over to Campbell's view. The Presbyterians promptly sold the rights to the Restoration Movement, who began printing and disseminating it!

Campbell made an intriguing case for the ministry of all believers. I think, personally, that is his greatest contribution. He was ingenious at calling us back to what truly is New Testament in that arena. Every person "in Christ Jesus" has been called into the ministry.

9. Acknowledge the lens of historical theology.

May I move to a slightly more delicate topic. One of the great claims of Campbell was that we worship without the accretions of church history or tradition. There is a lot of health in saying that. We certainly don't want to be like the Roman Catholic Church that says, "Our authority is found in the Scripture and in tradition." As Protestants, we are quite uncomfortable with that, particularly since Catholics seem to overtly use "tradition" to interpret Scripture.

But I would caution you that it's not as easy as one might think to jump from A.D. 95 to the present. You are who you are because of the lens of history.

Let me give you an example. We know so much more about justification by faith after Luther than we did before. We know more about the sovereignty of God after Calvin than before Calvin. We know so much more about walking in righteousness and holiness of life after Wesley than before. I'm so glad I live in the time I do. After these people, I can understand these subjects much better than I would have without them. So we really are products of the "development" of our faith. We cannot simply leap from biblical times to the present without honestly admitting that we have been shaped by the intervening centuries. We all have. It is important to admit that.

10. Keep reaching out to people like me.

I really want to affirm you on this. I admire your courage to do what you're doing. You see, my grandmother and my grandfather were members of an independent Christian church. I wish they would have invited me to church just once. I was very active in my church so perhaps they didn't want to pull me out of it. But I wish they would have brought me there so I would have known earlier the heritage that they shared. They were a part of the Restoration Movement. I wish they would have drawn me in and told me the stories.

Keep reaching out to enrich people like me at a more proactive level than what You have in the past. You make us better people. And I hope we impact you positively as well. I encourage you pastors to reach out more in your community. Go meet other pastors. Get more aggressive and proactive and cross-fertilize them with what you have to say.

I am amazed I did not know of the growth explosion of your group until recent years. My hat's off to you. But, you see, I know very little about you, except what I had "dug out" on Alexander Campbell on my own.

I know I'm not a part of the independent Christian church in a formal sense, but if you'll let me, I'll be a closet Campbellite!

PART SEVEN

LAST WILL AND TESTAMENT OF THE SPRINGFIELD PRESBYTERY

This document was signed at Cane Ridge, Kentucky, on June 28, 1804, by leaders of the Springfield Presbytery. This statement followed the pattern of a person's will as the signers sought to demonstrate their convictions about the church.

The Presbytery of Springfield sitting at Cane Ridge, in the county of Bourbon, being, through a gracious Providence, in more than ordinary bodily health, growing in strength and size daily; and in perfect soundness and composure of mind; but knowing that it is appointed for all delegated bodies once to die; and considering that the life of every such body is very uncertain, do make and ordain this our last Will and Testament, in manner and form following, viz.:

Imprimis. We will, that this body die, be dissolved, and sink into union with the Body of Christ at large; for there is but one body, and one Spirit, even as we are called in one hope of our calling.

Item. We will that our name of distinction, with its Reverend title, be forgotten, that there be but one Lord over God's heritage, and his name one.

Item. We will, that our power of making laws for the government of the church, and executing them by delegated authority, forever cease; that the people may have free course to the Bible, and adopt the law of the Spirit of life in Christ Jesus.

Item. We will, that candidates for the Gospel ministry henceforth study the Holy Scriptures with fervent prayer, and obtain license from God to preach the simple Gospel, with the Holy Ghost sent down from heaven, without any mixture of philosophy, vain deceit, traditions of men, or the rudiments of the world. And let none henceforth take this honor to himself, but he that is called of God, as was Aaron.

Item. We will, that the church of Christ resume her native right of internal government,—try her candidates for the ministry, as to their soundness in the faith, acquaintance with experimental religion, gravity and aptness to teach; and admit no other proof of their authority but Christ speaking in them. We will, that the church of Christ look up to the Lord of the harvest to send forth laborers into his harvest; and that she resume her primitive right of trying those who say they are apostles, and are not.

Item. We will, that each particular church, as a body, actuated by the same spirit, choose her own preacher, and support him by a free-will offering, without a written call or subscription—admit members—remove offenses; and never henceforth delegate her right of government to any man or set of men whatever.

Item. We will, that the people henceforth take the Bible as the only sure guide to heaven; and as many as are offended with other books, which stand in competition with it, may cast them into the fire if they choose; for it is better to enter into life having one book, than having many to be cast into hell.

Item. We will, that preachers and people cultivate a spirit of mutual forbearance; pray more and dispute less; and while they behold the signs of the times, look up, and confidently expect that redemption draweth nigh.

Item. We will, that our weak brethren, who may have been wishing to make the Presbytery of Springfield their king, and wot not what is now become of it, betake themselves to the Rock of Ages, and follow Jesus for the future.

Item. We will, the Synod of Kentucky examine every member who may be suspected of having departed from the Confession of Faith, and suspend every such suspected heretic immediately, in order that the oppressed may go free, and taste the sweets of Gospel liberty.

Item. We will, that Ja— ——-, the author of two letters lately published in Lexington, be encouraged in his zeal to destroy partyism. We will, moreover, that our past conduct be examined into by all who may have correct information; but let foreigners beware of speaking evil of things which they know not.

Item. Finally we will, that all our sister bodies read their Bibles carefully, that they may see their fate there determined, and prepare for death before it is too late.

Springfield Presbytery, June 28th, 1804

Robert Marshall,	}
John Dunlavy,	}
Richard M'Nemar,	}—Witnesses.
B. W. Stone,	}
John Thompson,	}
David Purviance,	}

PART EIGHT

COMMUNICATION METHODS

The following two lists have been used to accompany lectures on Communication Methods in the Restoration Movement. The first list indicates those methods common in the first century of the Movement. While most, if not all of them, continue to be used in the present, the second list adds many of the newer methods that have developed over the past 100 years.

Communication Methods Used in the Restoration Movement (1800-1900)
Church services
Discussions at home, work, traveling
Schools (by Christian teachers)
Colleges
Personal evangelism
Visual aids—"five finger exercise"
Revivals
Tracts
Debates
Conventions and lectureships
Periodicals
Sunday school curriculum
Books

Additional Communication Methods Used (1900—Present)
Christian service camps
Church planting groups
Local church newsletters/brochures/bulletins
Radio
Sermons
Specialized programs
Spot ads/commercials
Television
Cable productions
Films
Audio cassette tapes
Slides/filmstrips/16 mm motion pictures
Video
Videotapes
    In-church usage and loaning out

Satellite
House churches (especially overseas)
Telephone
Mass marketing/canvas calls
Inspirational messages
Music
Art—from chalk art to computer-generated
CDs and DVDs
Faxes
Newsletters/study guides
Campus ministry
Special interest groups
e.g. Motorcycle club/sports league/ham radio
Christian schools
Medical services and benevolence
Hospitals; homes for the aging, orphans, people with disabilities
Bookstores/reading rooms
Coffee houses/teen centers
Computers
    Web site, bulletin board, e-mail
Home and job-site Bible study groups

B I B L I O G R A P H Y

For more information on Restoration Movement History:

Garrett, Leroy. *The Stone-Campbell Movement.* Joplin, MO: College Press, 1981.

North, James B. *Union in Truth.* Cincinnati: Standard Publishing, 1994.

Richardson, Robert. *Memoirs of Alexander Campbell* (reprint ed.). Nashville: Gospel Advocate, 1956.

Thompson, Rhodes. *Voices from Cane Ridge.* St. Louis: Bethany Press, 1954.

For more information on Restoration Movement Principles:

Leggett, Marshall. *Introduction to the Restoration Ideal.* Cincinnati: Standard Publishing, 1986.

Shelly, Rubel. *I Just Want to Be a Christian.* Nashville: 20th-Century Christian, 1984.

Related Web Sites:

ACU, Restoration Studies **www.Bible.acu.edu/stone-campbell**

Christian Standard **www.christianstandard.com**

College Press **www.collegepress.com**

National Missionary Convention **www.nationalmissionaryconvention.org**

North American Christian Convention **www.nacctheconnectingplace.org**

Peace on Earth Ministries, *One Body* **www.poeministries.org**

World Convention **www.worldconvention.org**

Many Restoration Movement documents are available on the Web and can be located through any good search engine. (e.g., enter "*Our Position*" by Isaac Errett and you can find this shown on several sites.)

For Current Information:

Christian Church Today (a Web site serving Restoration Movement churches) **www.christianchurchtoday.com**

Directory of the Ministry (annual listing of churches, organizations, and personnel) Available from: 1525 Cherry Road, Springfield, IL 62704

College Press Online Directory (a Web page allowing access to detailed information on Christian Churches/Churches of Christ) **www.collegepress.com/ChurchDirectory/searchdirectory.aspx**